cLV

Werner Gitt

Questions

I Have Always
Wanted to Ask

Christliche Literatur-Verbreitung e. V.
Postfach 11 01 35 · 33661 Bielefeld

The Author, Werner Gitt was born in Raineck/East Prussia (Germany) in 1937. In 1963 he enrolled at the Technical University of Hanover and in 1968 he completed his engineering degree (Dipl.-Ing.). Thereafter he worked as an assistant at the Institute of Control Engineering at the Technical University of Aachen. Following two years of research work, he received his doctorate summa cum laude, together with the prestigious Borchers Medal from the Technical University of Aachen, Germany, in 1970. From 1971 to 2002 he was the Head of the Information Technology Division of the German Federal Institute of Physics and Technology (Physikalisch-Technische Bundesanstalt, PTB) in Braunschweig. In 1978 he was promoted to a Director and Professor at the PTB. He has written numerous scientific papers in the field of information science, numerical mathematics, and control engineering, as well as several popular books, some of which have been translated into more than 20 languages (e.g. Bulgarian, Chinese, Croatian, Czech, Dutch, English, Estonian, Finnish, French, Georgian, Hungarian, Italian, Japanese, Latvian, Lithuanian, Korean, Kyrgyz, Polish, Portuguese, Romanian, Swedish, Spanish, and Russian. Since 1984 he has been a regular guest lecturer at the State Independent Theological University of Basle, Switzerland, on the subject of 'Bible and Science'. He has held lectures on related topics at numerous universities at home and abroad, as well as having spoken on the topic 'Faith and Science' in a number of different countries (e.g. Australia, Austria, Belgium, Canada, France, Hungary, Japan, Kazakhstan, Kyrgyzstan, Lithuania, Namibia, Norway, Paraguay, Poland, Portugal, Romania, Russia, South Africa, Spain, Sweden, Switzerland, and the USA).

Homepage of Dr Werner Gitt: www.wernergitt.de
Here you will find:
• A listing of current speaking dates
• Essays and books in various languages for downloading
• Tracts in readable and printable format (e.g., "How can I get to Heaven?", "Who is the Designer?", "One-way journey", "What Darwin couldn't know", "… and He DOES exist", "The Greatest Invitation"), available for download in over 65 languages.

First English Edition 1992
Second Extended English Edition 1998
Third English Edition 2003
Fourth English Edition 2014

Translation of the First Edition: Marianne Rothe
Translation of the Extensions of the Second Edition: Dörte Götz
Corrections: Sarah Jayne Curtius, Dr Carl Wieland
Cover: Gerhard Thiessen, Bielefeld
Typography: CLV
Printed in Germany by BasseDruck GmbH, Hagen

CLV 255.184
ISBN 978-3-89397-184-8

Contents

Preface

How this book got started: The idea for this book originated during a number of evangelistic talks which the author held in the somewhat novel surroundings of the *Mühlhäuser* fashion house in Munich. Every night for a week, the couturier *Harro Mühlhäuser* allowed us to use the first floor of his business premises. This meant that every evening we had to take down clothes, remove racks, put out 250 chairs, give the talk, restack chairs, and put the racks up again so that the staff could rehang the clothes the following morning. There were nowhere near enough chairs, but the soft carpeting and the stairs served as additional comfortable seating. As a result we could easily seat 350 people. Being ideally situated in the mall in the middle of the CBD of Munich (within several metres of the City Hall and the Frauenkirche [Church of our Blessed Lady]) it attracted many from non-Christian circles. After the talk there was time for questions on the evening's topic. People made extensive use of this. The questions that were asked need to be answered before a decision on faith can be made.

Type of questions: As a result, this book contains many of the questions asked in Munich. In addition to these, it answers questions which were asked after similar talks at other localities. For a number of years now, the author has been in charge of the 'Question Hour in Krelingen' on 'Youth Day' (= Ahldener Jugendtag) in Krelingen (an evangelical centre in North Germany); in these sessions, also, numerous problems came up for discussion.

All the questions dealt with in this book have one thing in common – they are real questions, which were actually asked by someone. This is not a book giving the usual cross section of answers which Christian 'insiders' might expect. It tries instead to seriously address the problems which occupy the minds of those who are doubting, questioning and searching.

The author's experience of the questions put by seekers after his many lectures ensures that this is not some collection of hair-splitting theological or theoretical constructs, but rather deals with the fundamental issues with which real people are vitally concerned. A few of the more unusual questions the author has come across are also included.

Method of answering: The logic developed by the ancient Greeks has proved so successful in the exact sciences that one is tempted to transpose this way of thinking onto other areas as well. The Age of Reason was carried along by this type of logic, and the critical view of the Bible has been the result. If the questions dealt with in this book had been of a mathematical/scientific nature, then the calculus of logic would have been helpful. But the problems here at hand involve crucial, existential questions, the answers for which have generally evaded formal logical analysis. Nor is philosophy of any help to us here. The German philosopher from Karlsruhe, *Hans Lenk*, honestly admits:

> "Philosophy hardly ever gives final solutions with regard to content. It is a subject concerning problems, not matter and solution. It possibly considers a new problem perspective far more important than a partial solution to a given question."

God wants to and can lead us into all truth, in our mind as well as in our actions and matters of faith. Therefore, the crucial standard for us is the Word which has been authorized by God, which we know in the form of the Bible. This source of information cannot be replaced by any human product. Since the answers to these questions fundamentally depend on this standard, an extensive Appendix has been added, which deals with the nature of the Bible, and the principles for its interpretation. These fundamental principles have been compiled for the first time in this book and are meant to supply the basics which are necessary when dealing with the Bible.

For the sake of brevity, the answers are not always as exhaustive as they might have been; furthermore, a subjective selection of the numerous questions asked had to be made. As some questions are related to one another, the answers sometimes overlap. The questions have been subdivided into sections to make the outline easier to follow. Some questions can be answered directly from the Bible, since the answers are given explicitly there. Other questions can also be answered from the Bible, but only indirectly, by logical deduction from the biblical passages cited. The conclusions drawn in such fashion depend greatly on the author's depth of Bible knowledge and capacity for sound biblical reasoning, but are of necessity subjective. Questions as to 'why' remain, as a rule, unanswerable. These, too, will be answered one day (John 16:23). But only when faith is turned into sight.

Thanks: I would like to thank my dear wife for the helpful tips which she gave me while checking this manuscript through critical eyes and for taking on the laborious task of typing the manuscript into our home computer.

I pray that this book might be a help to many readers who are searching for answers concerning matters of life, death and faith.

Werner Gitt

Preface to the Second English Edition

I am delighted to see the English edition of this book once again in print. It is an improved, updated, and further developed version of the first edition. Chapter 7, dealing with heaven, is the most extensive addition. I would like to convey my thanks to *Dörte Götz*, MA, for the translation of all the additions. She has a degree in English and Russian translation from the University of Heidelberg. *Veronika Abraham*, pursuing studies towards a BA in History and Philosophy at Queen's University in Canada, also helped with translating the additions. *Sarah Jayne Curtius*, BA, was born in Britain and completed German and English language studies in Sheffield. She has reviewed the book stylistically, making refinements where necessary. I would like to thank them all for their thorough and committed work.

Finally, my friend *Dr Carl Wieland* (Australia) read the complete manuscript through again in context and made some further improvements. Dr Wieland is the director of the world-renowned organisation for creation science/research, *Answers in Genesis* in Brisbane (Australia). He is the editor of their brilliantly presented and colourful English-language magazine *Creation ex nihilo* magazine (print run > 50,000) which has subscribers in more than 120 countries. I am grateful to him as well for his efforts.

This book was first printed in Germany in 1989 and is now in its 15th edition, with 400,000 copies in all. It has become apparent to me, through many conversations with readers or letters that I have received, that many have found their way to faith in Jesus Christ with the help of this book. In the meantime, the book has been translated into 14 languages.

Werner Gitt, November 1998

1. Questions about God (QG)

QG 1: *How can I be sure that God really exists?*

AG 1: There is no nation or tribe in the world which does not, in one form or another, believe in a god, a spirit or a being which is superior to itself. This even applies to the most isolated jungle tribes who have never had contact with another culture, let alone heard the gospel. How is that possible? We all have the intellectual capacity to deduce from the wonderful visible creation which surrounds us that there is an invisible creator. Nobody believes that a car, a watch or even a button or a paper clip just happen. This is why Paul writes in the New Testament: "For since the creation of the world God's invisible qualities – his eternal power and divine nature – have been clearly seen, being understood from what has been made, so that men are without excuse" (Rom 1:20). Creation, however, only leads us to believe in the existence of a creator, allowing us to draw conclusions about His power and wealth of ideas, but not giving us any information as to His nature (e.g. love, life, mercy, goodness). The Bible has been given to us for this purpose.

QG 2: *Where is God?*

AG 2: We humans try to localize God. This is why we find so much on this in the heathen concepts of gods in ancient times as well as in neo-paganism. The Greeks believed that their gods lived on the mountain Olympus while the Teutons placed their gods in Valhalla. The French mathematician and astronomer *P. Laplace* (1749–1827) said: "I have searched the whole of space, but I didn't find God anywhere." Soviet cosmonauts commented in a similar vein: "I didn't meet God during my flight" (*Nikolajew*, 1962, in Wostok III). Scripturally, all of these statements are fundamentally wrong because God is outside our dimensions. He who has created space cannot be part of our dimensions. What is more, He permeates every part of space, He is omnipresent. Paul explains this to the heathen Athenians on the Areopagus: "For in him [God] we live and move and have our being" (Acts 17:28). The psalmist, too, knows this to be a reality when he confesses: "You discern my going out and my lying down; you hem me in – you have laid your hand upon me" (Ps 139:3,5). This, too, shows how completely God surrounds and permeates our world. The mathematical idea of extra-dimensional space (our space has three dimensions) can assist with the question of where God is. n-dimensional space is only a subset of $(n+1)$-dimensional space. Similarly, four-dimensional space, for example, cannot be understood by three-dimensional space, but it still permeates it completely. Scripture illustrates this when it says in 1 Kings 8:27: "But will God really dwell on earth? The heavens, even the highest heaven, cannot contain you."

QG 3: *What does the word God – G.O.D. – mean?*

AG 3: The word *God* is not an acronym, i.e. a word formed from the initial letters of a group of words such as UFO (**u**nidentified **f**lying **o**bject). God has revealed Himself to man through ever new names, which describe the nature of God (the following scriptures indicate the first time the particular name appears):

elohim	(Gen 1:1; God – plural, in order to express the trinity of Father, Son and Holy Spirit)
eloah	(41 times in the book of Job, otherwise scattered, God – singular of elohim)
el	(Gen 33:20; God, the all powerful)

el-olam	(Gen 21:33; eternal God)
el-shaddai	(Gen 17:1; all-powerful God)
el-roi	(Gen 16:13 God who sees me)
jahweh	(Gen 2:4; according to Exodus 3:15 *I am who I am*)
jahweh-rapheka	(Ex 15:26, the Lord who heals you)
jahweh-nissi	(Ex 17:15, the Lord my banner)
jahweh-jireh	(Gen 22:13-14, the Lord will provide)
jahweh-shalom	(Judges 6:24, the Lord is peace)
jahweh-zidkenu	(Jer 23:6, the Lord our righteousness)
jahweh-shammah	(Ez 48:35, the Lord is there)
jahweh-roi	(Ps 23:1, the Lord my shepherd)
jahweh-zebaoth	(God of the armies)
adonai	(Gen 15:2, my Lord, 134 times in the OT).

(Ref. *Abraham Meister*, 'Biblisches Namenlexikon' [Biblical lexicon of names], Pfäffikon, 1970)

QG 4: *Why can't we see God?*

AG 4: The first couple created by God, Adam and Eve, lived in communion with Him and saw Him face to face. Because of the Fall man was separated from God. He is a holy God who hates all sin and this is why the original closeness came to an end. "[God] lives in inapproachable light, whom no-one has seen or can see" (1 Tim 6:16). This is why we will not see Him until we enter the Father's house after our death. The way to Him is open only through Jesus Christ: "No-one comes to the Father except through me" (John 14:6).

QG 5: *Can God be a God of love if He permits all this misery in the world? Why does God allow suffering?*

AG 5: Prior to the Fall (Gen 3), there was neither death nor suffering, neither pain nor any of that which causes us such problems today. God had created everything in such a way that man could live under ideal conditions. Of his own free will man decided to follow his own path, which led him away from God. Why God grants us such a wide spectrum of freedom is something we cannot explain. However, we see that to turn our back on God is to end in misery. Bitter experience shows us this even today. Some people tend to blame God. But we should remember that it is we, mankind, who are responsible, not God. If we travel on the highway at night, switch off the headlights and cause an accident as a result, we cannot blame the car manufacturer. He supplied the headlights as a source of light. If we deliberately switch them off, then that is our responsibility. "God is light" (1 John 1:5), and when we move into the darkness of separation from God we cannot complain to the Creator who had made us to live close to Him. God is and remains a God of love because He did something unimaginable: He gave His own Son in order to redeem us from a situation for which we alone are responsible. Jesus said of Himself in John 15:13: "Greater love has no-one than this, that lay down his life for his friends." Is there a greater love? Never has anything greater been done for man than on that day on Calvary: The cross is hence the highlight of divine love.

All of us – whether believer or unbeliever – live in a fallen world. Suffering, with all the manifestations so well-known to us, forms an integral part of this world. Individual suffering remains incomprehensible to us. Why is one person well off while the other is hard-hit by calamities and serious illness? Often the believer has to suffer more than the unbeliever. The psalmist records:

> "For I envied the arrogant when I saw the prosperity of the wicked. They have no struggles; their bodies are healthy and strong. They are free from the burdens common to man; they are not plagued by human ills" (Ps 73:3-5).

He does, however, correctly rate his individual suffering, realizing that it is not a punishment for his sin. He does not quarrel with God, but clings to Him:

> "Yet I am always with you; you hold me by my right hand. You guide me with your counsel, and afterwards you will take me into glory. My flesh and my heart may fail, but God is the strength of my heart and my portion for ever" (Ps 73:23-24,26).

QG 6: *Isn't God to blame for everything?*

AG 6: When God called Adam to account after the Fall, Adam pointed at Eve: "The woman you put here with me – she gave me some fruit from the tree, and I ate it" (Gen 3:12). When God then spoke to Eve, she, too, passed the blame on to someone else: "The serpent deceived me, and I ate" (Gen 3:13). In matters of sin, we exhibit strange behaviour: we always point away from ourselves until eventually we declare God to be the guilty one. Now, however, the inconceivable happens: in Jesus, God bears all the blame: "God made him [Jesus] who had no sin to be sin for us" (2 Cor 5:21). God's judgment on the sin of the world focuses on the Son of God. The anathema is hurled against Him in all its power, the entire land is plunged into darkness for three hours at His crucifixion, He is truly forsaken by God. "[He] gave himself for our sins" (Gal 1:4) so that we can be free. This is how God's love manifests itself. There are no gladder tidings than the gospel.

QG 7: *In Old Testament times God wiped out an entire nation by means of wars while in the Sermon on the Mount it says* love your enemies. *Is the God of the OT (Old Testament) different to the God of the NT (New Testament)?*

AG 7: Some people consider the God of the OT to be a God of wrath and revenge and the God of the NT a God of love. This opinion is easily disproved by the following two statements from the OT and the NT: In Jeremiah 31:3 God says: "I have loved you with an everlasting love; I have drawn you with loving-kindness", and in the NT we read in Hebrews 10:31: "It is a dreadful thing to fall into the hands of the living God." God is a God of wrath when confronted with sin and a loving God when confronted by the contrite. We find this testimony in both the OT and the NT because God is always the same. He "does not change like shifting shadows" (James 1:17). In the same way, the Son of God never changes: "Jesus Christ is the same yesterday and today and for ever" (Hebr 13:8).

Scripture is full of examples showing how, on the one hand, the Lord condemns the sins of people and how, on the other hand, He protects His children. During the flood, all of mankind outside the Ark drowned because of its wickedness and only eight people were saved. Similarly, the majority of mankind will perish during the Final Judgment because they trod the broad road of destruction (Matt 7:13-14). God gave the Promised Land into the hands of His nation Israel, but during the exodus from Egypt the Amalekites attacked those who were lagging behind. In Deuteronomy 25:17-19 God announces to the Amalekites that they will be destroyed, which Saul did later on the command of the Lord (1 Sam 15:3). In NT times, Ananias and Sapphira are killed by God because they did not tell the entire truth (Acts 5:1-11). These examples teach us that God sees sin in a more serious light than we think. In that, too, God has never changed. He hates all sin and He will judge every misdeed. He could still destroy entire nations today. The Germans, for example, have sinned against God in a particularly serious way because of the programme to exterminate His nation Israel, developed in their nation during the Third Reich. The division of Germany for 40 years and the loss of the eastern sections were an obvious judgment. God could have destroyed the entire nation, but His mercy was so great that He did not do so, possibly because of the believers that still exist. Sodom and Gomorrha would not have been destroyed had there been at least ten righteous men (Gen 18:32). If judgment does not take place immediately it is due to God's mercy. But the time will come when everyone will have to give account of his/her life, believers (2 Cor 5:10) as well as unbelievers (Hebr 9:27; Rev 20:11-15).

QG 8: *Did God create evil?*

AG 8: In 1 John 1:5 we read that God is light. "In him there is no darkness at all." God is absolutely pure and perfect (Matt 5:48) and the angels testify: "Holy holy holy is the LORD Almighty" (Is 6:3). He is the Father of light (James 1:17), and therefore evil could never originate in Him. The origins of evil, the Bible tells us, are connected to the fall of Satan who was once a cherub, an angel of light, and wanted to be "like the Most High" (Is 14:14). In Ezekiel 28:15ff his pride and fall are recounted:

"You were blameless in your ways from the day you were created till wickedness was found in you. Through your widespread trade you were filled with violence, and you sinned. So I drove you in disgrace from the mount of God, and I expelled you, O guardian cherub, from among the fiery stones. Your heart became proud ... So I threw you to the earth."

Because the first people gave in to temptation they became slaves to sin. Thus, evil found its way into creation, and Satan became lord of this world. "For our struggle is not against flesh and blood, but against the rulers, against the authorities,

against the powers of this dark world and against the spiritual
forces of evil in the heavenly realms" (Eph 6:12).

QG 9: *Is God capable of learning something new?*

AG 9: To learn is, by definition, to take in previously unknown
facts. Since God knows all things (Ps 139:2; John 16:30), there is
nothing new for Him to learn. As master over space and time,
the past as well as the future is known to Him. We, however,
remain on a learning curve. In His omniscience, the Lord tells
us in Scripture of coming events by means of prophecies.

QG 10: *Did Jesus really live? Is He the Son of God?*

AG 10: The foretelling of Jesus' coming into this world
forms part of the most convincing of the Bible's prophetic
statements. At great length, the OT prophesies His place
of birth (Micah 5:1 \ Luke 2:4), His genealogy (2 Sam 7:16 \
Matt 1:1-17), the simultaneous father-son relationship with
God (Ps 2:7; 2 Sam 7:14 \ Hebr 1:5) and with man (Dan 7:13
\ Luke 21:27), His ministry (Is 42:7 \ John 9), the reason for
His mission (Is 53:4-5 \ Mark 10:45), the betrayal for 30 pieces
of silver (Zech 11:12 \ Matt 26:15), His suffering and death
on the cross (Ps 22 \ Luke 24:26) and His resurrection (Hos
6:2 \ Luke 24:46). The marked interval of 400 years between
the last book of the OT and the beginning of the NT narration gives a particularly impressive significance to the fulfilled
prophecies about Christ in connection with the question asked
above. There are also non-biblical sources testifying to the
life of Jesus such as the Roman historian *Tacitus*, the Roman
court official *Sueton* under the Emperor *Hadrian*, the Roman
governor of Bithynia in Asia Minor, *Thallus*, and others. As an
example, let me cite the well-known Jewish historian *Flavius
Josephus* (born 37 AD):

"Now, there was about this time Jesus, a wise man, if it be lawful to call him a man, for he was a doer of wonderful works, a teacher of such men as receive the truth with pleasure. He drew over to him both many of the Jews, and many of the Gentiles. He was (the) Christ. And when Pilate, at the suggestion of the principal men amongst us, had condemned him to the cross, those that loved him at the first did not forsake him; for he appeared to them alive again the third day; as the divine prophets had foretold these and ten thousand other wonderful things concerning him. And the tribe of Christians, so named from him, are not extinct at this day."

('Antiquities of the Jews', Volume II, p 412; Oxford, printed by *D. A. Talboys*, 1839).

God Himself confirms that Jesus is His Son (during the baptism: Matt 3:17; on the mount of transfiguration: Mark 9:7) and the angel announces His birth as *Son of the Most High* (Luke 1:32). The Lord Jesus professes to be God's son during the trial before the Sanhedrin, the supreme legislative council and the highest ecclesiastical and secular tribunal in Israel, composed of high priests, elders and teachers of the law, presided over by the chief priest Caiphas (Mt 26:63-64; Mk 14:61-62; Lk 22:70). Various other men and women also attest that Jesus is the son of God:

- Peter: "You are the Christ, the Son of the living God" (Matt 16:16).

- John: "If anyone acknowledges that Jesus is the Son of God, God lives in him and he in God" (1 John 4:15).

- Paul: "I live by faith in the Son of God" (Gal 2:20).

- Martha: "I believe that you are the Christ, the Son of God, who was to come into the world" (John 11:27).

- Nathanael: "Rabbi, you are the Son of God" (John 1:49).

- the Roman centurion: "Surely he was the Son of God" (Matt 27:54).

- the Ethiopian treasurer: "I believe that Jesus Christ is the Son of God" (Acts 8:37).

The devil, too, knows about the kinship between God, the Father, and Jesus Christ, the Son (Matt 4:3,6), and the demons have to acknowledge Him as the Son of God (Matt 8:29).

The Pharisees and High Priests took great offence at the fact that Jesus was the Son of God (Mark 14:53-65) as did the incited mob (John 19:7). To the Jews and Muslims Jesus is still a thorn in the flesh today. He could not, however, be our Saviour and Redeemer if he were only a "brother" (*Shalom ben Chorin*), "Son among Sons" (German theologian *Heinz Zahrnt*), a godly man or a social reformer. He is our Saviour and Redeemer because truly he is the Son of the living God (Matt 16:16).

QG 11: *What is the relationship between God and Jesus? Are they one person, or which of the two is higher in status? To whom should we pray?*

AG 11: God cannot be grasped by our minds. He is outside our dimension, non-temporal and unfathomable. This is why in the first Commandment all pictorial images of Him are forbidden. God, however, has not "left himself without testimony" (Acts 14:17), He has revealed Himself to us. He is *One* and at the same time the *Trinity*.

1. *God is One.* There is no other God but the God of Abraham, Isaac and Jacob (Ex 3:6): "I am the first and I am the last; apart from me there is no God" (Is 44:6). "Before me no god was formed, nor will there be one after me. I, even I, am the

LORD, and apart from me there is no saviour" (Is 43:10-11). "You shall have no other gods before me" (Ex 20:3). The Gods of other religions are null and void: "For all the gods of the nations are idols" (Ps 96:5), "there images are but wind and confusion" (Is 41:29).

2. *God is the Trinity:* At the same time, we encounter God as the triune, three-persons-in-one God of the Trinity. This does not mean three Gods but – as documented in many passages in the Bible (for example 1 Cor 12:4-6; Eph 1:17; Hebr 9:14) – a threefold harmony of the will, action and nature of God. We talk about this triune God in three different ways, describing different persons: God, the Father; Jesus Christ, the Son of God; the Holy Spirit. This is at its most explicit and most obvious during the call to baptism according to Matthew 28:19. The expression "the Trinity" (Lat. *trinitas* = threefold), which is mentioned nowhere in the Bible, is a human attempt at conceptualizing this divine mystery in one word.

In **Jesus** God became man: "The Word became flesh" (John 1:14). God became visible, audible, touchable (1 John 1:1) and tangible by faith (John 6:69). God sent us the Lord Jesus Christ and "God presented him [to be received] through faith" (Rom 3:25). Therefore Jesus has a special task to fulfil for us. Our faith becomes a saving faith only if we believe in Jesus Christ as our Redeemer and Lord. He went to the cross for us, He atoned for our sin, our redemption cost him dearly (1 Pet 1:18). This is why we call on Him alone to be saved (Rom 10:13). We have gained access to the Father through him (John 14:6) and, as children, may call Him "Abba, dear Father" (Rom 8:15). Jesus is the Son of God, His nature is the same as God's. "I and the Father are one" (John 10:30). This is why he could say: "Anyone who has seen me has seen the Father" (John 14:9). Faced by the resurrected Jesus, Thomas admits: "My Lord and my God" (John 20:28). Jesus is divine and His nature is the same as the Father's. This is also expressed by

the following identical titles and actions: Creator (Is 40:28 \
John 1:3), light (Is 60:19-20 \ John 8:12), shepherd (Ps 23:1 \
John 10:11), first and last (Is 41:4 \ Rev 1:17), forgiver of sins
(Jer 31:34 \ Mark 2:5), Creator of the angels (Ps 148:5 \ Col
1:16), adored by angels (Ps 148:2 \ Hebr 1:6). Philippians 2:6
also stresses the sameness of Jesus with the Father. When
He became man, He took on the likeness of a human servant.
Now He was in total dependence on, and in obedience to, the
Father. In this context – Jesus becoming human – a clear order
of rank between Father and Son becomes apparent: "As man is
the head of the woman, so God is the head of Christ" (1 Cor
11:3). But now the Lord Jesus is seated to the right of God
and is the exact representation of His being (Hebr 1:3). The
Father has given the Son all authority in heaven and on earth
(Matt 28:18). The judgment, too, has been entrusted to the
Son (John 5:22) since He has given everything in subjection
to Christ (1 Cor 15:27). Finally, it is said: "When he has done
this [= given everything under Christ] then the Son himself
will be made subject to him who put everything under him, so
that God may be all in all" (1 Cor 15:28).

We encounter the **Holy Spirit**, likewise, as a divine person,
but he fulfils different tasks to those of the Son of God. He is
our comforter (John 14:26) and representative before God,
he opens our eyes to the truth of the Bible (John 14:17), he
intercedes for us before God (Rom 8:26), and without him,
we could not even recognize Jesus as our Saviour and Lord
(1 Cor 12:3b).

Prayer: Jesus taught His disciples, and so us as well, how to
pray to the Father (Matt 6:9-13). When the Apostle John fell
to the ground before the power of the angel and wanted to
worship him, the messenger of God strictly forbids this: "I am a
fellow servant with you … Worship God" (Rev 22:9). Similarly,
the prayer to Jesus is not just possible and desirable but, since
His Coming into the world, a command. He Himself said to

the disciples: "Until now you have not asked for anything in my name" (John 16:24) and "You may ask me for anything in my name, and I will do it" (John 14:14). Colossians 3:17 admonishes us to pray in the name of the Lord Jesus: "And whatever you do, whether in word or deed, do it all in the name of the Lord Jesus, giving thanks to God the Father through him." Jesus is the only mediator between God and man (1 Tim 2:5) and this is why we may turn to Him in prayer. The first martyr, Stephen, is described to us as an exemplary man "full of the Holy Spirit" (Acts 7:55). His prayer while being stoned by an angry mob has been recorded as "Lord Jesus, receive my spirit" (Acts 7:59). Even while the Lord Jesus lived on earth, He was worshipped as God, which He did not reject: the man with leprosy (Matt 8:2), the man born blind (John 9:38) and the disciples (Matt 14:33) all bowed down and acknowledged Him as their Lord. This, according to the Scriptures, is the most explicit sign of worship and adoration. There is no scriptural reference, however, to a prayer to the Holy Spirit (as for example in the hymn 'O Holy Ghost, to Thee we all pray for true faith' by *Berthold von Regensburg*).

According to the Bible, prayer can only be adressed to God, the Father, or to Jesus Christ, His Son.

2.   Questions about the Bible (QB)

The following set of questions, dealing as it does with the validity and reliability of the Bible, is of a very fundamental nature. Thus, only five questions are dealt with in this chapter, and – as befits the importance of this subject – a very detailed appendix has been added.

QB 1: *The Bible was written by people: doesn't this make everything relative? How can you say that the Bible is from God and that everything in it is true?*

AB 1: We will answer this question concerning scriptural truth by means of a specific example, which has the advantage of being mathematically reproducible. The Bible contains 6,408 verses with prophetic statements, of which 3,268 have come to pass while the remaining prophecies concern future events. No fulfilment of a prophecy differed from the way it was described. This has not been equalled by any other book in world history. What we have here is a truth quota – also expressible in mathematical formulae – which has no equal anywhere else. We now want to ask: is it possible that so many prophecies came to pass by coincidence? i.e. can their fulfilment be explained without the intervention of God? In considering these questions, let us use a probability formula. In the calculation model below, two things have been ignored, namely that sometimes several verses in the Bible describe a single prophecy while, on the other hand, one verse sometimes contains several prophecies. Similarly, the fact that some prophecies are mentioned several times is not included in the calculation. This simplification of the model is compensated for, however, by the following formulation for the basic probability.

If one assumes the very high basic probability of $p = 0.5$ for the *chance* fulfilment of a single prophecy, then the overall probability w for the 3,268 prophecies which have come to pass already can be accurately calculated. This is $w = 2^{-3268} = 1.714 \times 10^{-984}$. The prophecies are actually such that the chances of their occurring as described can be formulated mathematically to be from $1 : 1,000$ to $1 :$ several millions. With the formulation $1 : 2 (= 0.5)$ we would thus certainly err on the safe side. To compare numbers for w let us look at several imaginary lottery systems. Taking the probability for a 'jackpot' in the commercial '6 in 49' number lottery (i.e. 6 correct numbers in 49 blocks with consecutive numbering) as about $1 : 14$ million, let us then ask: How many more blocks would we need to add onto another lottery ticket (where 6 correct numbers would also be a 'jackpot') in order for the probability of winning on such a ticket to be the same as that for the chance fulfilment of 3,268 prophecies? What would we estimate the size of such a ticket to be?

a) the size of a table tennis table?
   On an area of $A = 1.525 \times 2.74$ m^2 = 4.1785 m^2, the number of blocks (L) of the same size as on a standard commercial lottery ticket which could be accommodated would be 167,140 blocks.

b) the size of a soccer field?
   Where $A = 7,350$ m^2, L would be 459,375,000 blocks.

c) or even the surface of the entire earth?
   If $A = 510$ million km^2, L would be 31.3653×10^{18} blocks, where 10^{18} is a quintillion or a million million million.

If one were to calculate the probabilities of having six correct numbers for L number of blocks, then the probability (w) in each of the above examples would be as follows:

a) $w = 1 : 0.4 \times 10^{30}$ (or 2.5×10^{-30})
b) $w = 1 : 1.3 \times 10^{49}$ (or 7.69×10^{-50})
c) $w = 1 : 1.3 \times 10^{114}$ (or 7.69×10^{-115})

The numbers for w show that the comparisons a) to c) are totally inadequate. The mathematical result for the number of blocks is absolutely breathtaking. In order to have an adequate comparison, we would need to contemplate the total number of atoms in the universe and this, being 10^{80}, is in itself no longer imaginable (it is a 1 with 80 zeros, or ten thousand million multiplied by itself eight times). To try to comprehend the calculated trans-astronomical figure of 2.74×10^{164} blocks needed for that super lottery ticket, one would have to use a comparison which exceeds our imagination even further: imagine as many universes of the same size as our universe has atoms, then the *total number of atoms of all of these imaginary universes* would still be smaller, by a factor of 27,400, than the number of extra blocks required on that lottery ticket! [G1, p 139].

In light of the above considerations, only one conclusion is possible: the prophecies are divine, their origin cannot be human. Thus, the calculation leads us to a result which Jesus, in the well known prayer to His Father often described as the High Priestly prayer (incorrectly so, since it does not involve a High Priestly service, i.e. the atonement of the nation's sins) condenses to the compact formulation, "Your word is truth" (John 17:17). The Scriptures can therefore not be of human origin; on the contrary: "All Scripture is God-breathed" (2 Tim 3:16). God used selected people to whom He gave important information so that they – without excluding their personality, their nature and their emotions – could record this for us. Additional information concerning this question can be found in three sub-sections of part 1 ('Fundamental Principles of the Bible') of the Appendix: I.1 The Origin of the Bible; I.2 The Truth Content of the Bible; I.3 Testing Biblical Truths.

QB 2: *How can I find out whether the Bible is true?*

AB 2: Whether, given specific conditions, a mathematically formulated, physical process or a particular chemical reaction will occur or not is not determined by a panel discussion, but by repeatable experiment. In contrast to all other writings of various ideologies and religions, the Bible names methods of proving its truth empirically. Those whose questions are not purely of a philosophical nature, but are really searching for an answer are invited to take part in an experiment, for which God Himself will vouch.

> "Do not let this Book of the Law depart from your mouth; meditate on it day and night, so that you may be careful to do everything written in it. Then you will be prosperous and successful." (Or from the Hebrew: "Then you will be able to act wisely and succeed in all your undertakings" (Jos 1:8).

This experiment thus consists of three steps:

1. *Getting to know the specifications of the experiment:* First of all we need to become familiar with the contents of the Bible by reading it diligently.

2. *Implementing the experiment:* Secondly, all recognized instructions need to be put into practice.

3. *Testing of the experimental data:* Everybody desires a successful life in the areas of marriage and family, profession and leisure time. The questions put to counsellors in the tabloid press provide sufficient evidence. No psychological marriage counsellor, no industrial manager and no political consultant has an ultimate recipe for success up his sleeve. Only the Bible promises success and wise actions if the above conditions are met.

Those who carry out this experiment always arrive at a positive conclusion. There is neither loss nor risk. Unlike the stakes you lose in a lottery or the interest you have to pay on a loan, with this experiment you lose nothing. If you dare to take the Bible at its word you are dealing with God and your gain will be enormous. (Further possibilities for testing the truth of the Bible are included in the Appendix 'Annotations to the Bible', Part I.2. 'The Biblical Truths').

QB 3: *In what respects does the Bible differ from other books of world literature?*

AB 3: The Bible differs fundamentally from other books of world literature in several respects as it represents a unique, singular and incomparable work:

1. *Despite having been written over a span of 1,000 years, Scripture possesses a unique continuity:* The Bible was written by approximately 45 writers of different backgrounds and professions. Among the writers are for example the university graduate Moses, the military commander-in-chief Joshua, the prime minister Daniel, the cupbearer Nehemiah, King David, the shepherd Amos, the fisherman Peter, the customs officer Matthew, the doctor Luke and the tent maker Paul. The various portions of the Bible were written in unusual places such as the desert (Moses), in jail (Jeremiah), in a palace (Daniel), on tour (Luke) or in exile (John) and marked by every imaginable emotion of the writers such as joy and love, fear and anxiety, suffering and despair. Despite the time span of 60 generations, which is not to be found in any other such work, and the different social levels of its authors, the Bible is characterized by uniformity and harmony in all subject matters. The writers deal with hundreds of topics in a way that is conspicuously harmonious and consistent. Experience shows that if men from such remote eras with divergent personalities were to deal with such a spectrum of topics without the intervention of God, no such unity could be expected. In particular, God and His plan for salvation run through the Bible like a scarlet thread.

2. *Scripture is made up of a wide scope of literary genres not to be found in any other book* (see Principle P58 in Appendix, Part I). On the other hand, those genres clearly connected with fiction such as fairy tales, legends and sagas are excluded. Also excluded are exaggerations or understatements usually found in satires, glosses, epics or comedies.

3. *The Bible is characterized by remarkable diversity*. It is a book about faith, law and history all at the same time. It supplies the foundations for numerous disciplines and contains thousands of guidelines for day-to-day situations. It is the best marriage counsellor available and shows how we should interact with parents and children, friends and enemies, neighbours and relatives, strangers, guests and fellow-believers (for more on this see question QL 3). It deals with the origin of this world and of all life, the nature of death and the end of the world. It shows us the nature of God, the Father, His Son Jesus Christ and the workings of the Holy Spirit.

4. *The Bible is the only book which contains absolutely trustworthy prophecies*. These are of divine origin (1 Sam 9:9; 2 Sam 24:11; 2 Pet 1:20-21) and thus cannot be found in any other book of world literature (neither in the Qur'an nor in the writings of the French occultist *Nostradamus*). The time lapse between the actual writing of each prophecy and its fulfilment is so great that not even the most severe critic could claim that the prophecies had not been given until the events had already taken place (see [G1, pp. 118-148]).

5. *The time frame of biblical testimony has no equal:* The Bible extends from the origin of the physical time axis (creation) to its conclusion (Rev 20:6b). No other book records with any certainty the beginnings of time nor can it describe the end of time with any accuracy. Furthermore, the Bible talks about eternity, the reality in which our restrictive temporal laws are no longer valid.

6. *No assertion of the Bible has yet been proved incorrect*. No scientific references in the Bible have ever been revised due to research results. On the contrary, there are numerous examples of biblical scientific descriptions being confirmed by research many centuries later (e.g. the number of stars [G7, pp. 15-23], shape of the earth [G1, pp. 59-60]).

7. *No other book describes man as realistically as the Bible*. There are no comic exaggerations, no touched-up biographies and no glorified heroism, which hide or veil the negative aspects of man. This is why, for instance, the sins of the patriarchs in the Bible (Gen 12:11-13), the adultery of David (2 Sam 11) and the disorder in the congregations (1 Cor 1:11; 2 Cor 2:1-4) are not omitted.

8. *The Bible describes future events unimaginable for the people of that time* (e.g. space labs, orbit stations: Obadiah 4). It includes situations in its teaching which were to occur many centuries later (such as drug abuse, 2 Cor 6:16-17; gene technology, see question QL 10).

The eight characteristics mentioned above show the Bible to be a unique book, incomparable to any other. The historian *Philip Schaff* testifies to the uniqueness of the Scriptures and to the One of whom it speaks very aptly:

"This Jesus of Nazareth, without money and arms, conquered more millions than Alexander, Caesar, Mohammed and Napoleon; without science and learning, he shed more light on things human and divine than all philosophers and scholars combined; without the eloquence of schools, he spoke such words of life as were never spoken before or since and produced effects, which lie beyond the reach of orator or poet. Without writing a single line, he set more pens in motion and furnished themes for more sermons, orations, discussions, learned volumes, works of art and songs of praise than the whole army of great men of ancient and modern times" (*Josh McDowell*, 'Evidence that Demands a Verdict', p 137).

Although Scripture can be quantified exactly with regard to the number of words and letters (e.g. *King James Version* 783,137 words and 3,566,489 letters), the wealth of its ideas is infinite. No life is long enough to exhaust all its thoughts (Ps 119:162). We can thus read the Bible as often as we like and it will never be boring. Every time we reread a passage, new ideas and cross-references to other texts come to mind. This leads us come to an important conclusion: the Bible is the only divine book. Its truth has been guaranteed and authorized by God (Ps 119:160; John 17:17).

QB 4: *Are there new messages today that supplement the Bible? Surely God is greater than Scripture and He can communicate directly?*

AB 4: We have to differentiate between two different divine ways of communication: the Bible, which is valid for everyone, and the Lord's guidance in each individual life.

1. Supplements to the Bible? False prophets with their own unauthorized messages were present alongside the men who were called and authorized by God to write the Bible (e.g. Jer 1:5; Gal 1:12). God answers the topical question of "How can we know when a message has been spoken by the Lord?" (Deut 18:21) by providing crucial criteria for testing the truth:

"If what a prophet proclaims in the name of the LORD does not take place or come true, that is a message the LORD has not spoken. That prophet has spoken presumptuously" (Deut 18:22).

In the Sermon on the Mount Jesus also warns of false prophets and gives characteristics for their identification:

"Watch out for false prophets. They come to you in sheep's clothing, but inwardly they are ferocious wolves. By their fruit you will recognise them. Do people pick grapes from thornbushes, or figs from thistles?" (Matt 7:15-16).

The Apostle John writes of this danger in no less compelling terms: "Many deceivers … have gone out into the world. … Anyone who runs ahead and does not continue in the teaching of Christ does not have God" (2 John 7,9).

The Bible is God's revelation. God spoke through his Son (Hebr 1:2) and there will be no further revelations (Rev 22:18). Nothing may be added to the words of the Bible. Even in his day, Peter warned of "destructive heresies" (2 Pet 2:1), which lead men to ruin. The additions to and perversion of the Bible by *Joseph Smith* (Book of Mormon), *Jakob Lorbeer* (Friends of the Neo-Revelation), *Ch. T. Russel* (Jehovah's Witnesses) *J.G. Bischoff* (New-Apostolic), *Mary Baker Eddy* (Christian Science) and others are not divine messages, but tragic lies by false teachers and seducers. God does not give supplementary revelations, but only sheds new light on that which He has already given in the OT and the NT. Thus the Bible remains the only binding source of information and the only standard whereby everything is to be verified. Statements by our contemporaries which start off with "the Lord has told me…" also need to be stringently tested, for the reasons mentioned above.

2. Individual guidance by God: So often we wish we could have God speak into specific situations. God could do this, but as a rule He does not. *Martin Luther, John Wesley, Hudson Taylor* or *Billy Graham* were or are important men of God who accomplished extraordinary things. They relied on the Word of God and received impulses for their blessed ministries from there. Our prayer "Teach me your way, O LORD" (Ps 86:11) seeks God's intervention in our lives. This can be experienced and becomes God's clear intervention often only in hindsight, but as a rule it happens silently without God's audible voice.

QB 5: *What do you make of* Michael Drosnin's *Bible Code?*

AB 5: The American journalist *Michael Drosnin* claims in his book 'The Bible Code' (Weidenfeld & Nicolson, Great Britain, 1997) that the Bible contains a hidden code that has now been cracked. First, the 304,805 letters of the original Hebrew text of the 5 books of Moses are saved in a computer, in their original order, leaving out the blank spaces. Then every 'nth' letter is taken from this sequence (for example with the interval n = 2, 3, 4 or 17, 35 and so on), thus repeatedly producing new letter sequences. The number of sequences can be increased by frame-shifting, i.e. by not starting with the first letter, but any other. In addition, the linear sequences thus obtained are arrayed in blocks, the spacing of which can vary at will, thus drastically increasing the number of possible letter combinations. One then searches for words or word-fragments that have a significant meaning, into which one can interpret 'prophecies' for our time. What are we to make of this method?

Information-theoretical Objections:
1. This method is completely arbitrary. It is inevitable that in such a large, virtually inexhaustible supply of letters,

meaningful names and words will be found. The chances are drastically increased by looking for words not just horizontally, but also vertically and diagonally within a block. Besides which, one is allowed to read in all directions – from right to left and vice versa, as well as from top to bottom and vice versa. Further: within one particular search, *Drosnin* randomly changes the method of reading to produce even more fitting words of association. Word 1 is read for example from right to left, word 2 from top to bottom, but only every second letter is taken. The variables of the diagonals should not be forgotten either.

2. It should be kept in mind that by far the largest part of the sequences of letters is merely junk, in which even allowing many different ways of reading, no meaningful elements can be found. In addition, if you take into consideration the peculiarity of the Hebrew language, in which some vowels are not written, the likelihood of finding meaningful words or word fragments is considerably higher.

3. According to the Bible Code method, the symbols are always drawn from the same source. Therefore, the distribution of the frequency of letters (which reflects written Hebrew) remains constant. Thus, the occurrence of words in the Hebrew language by chance is more probable than in a pool with a different (e.g. random) distribution of frequency of Hebrew letters.

4. *Drosnin* chose the name 'Bible Code' for his statistical game but this is a misnomer. A code always requires the existence of a sender or originator [G5, pp. 67-80]. As shown above, the combinations of letters resulting from *Drosnin's* method are the results of pure chance. Random results cannot be decoded, because, by definition, they carry no meaning. With that, everything that *Drosnin* tries to read is purely arbitrary, is completely unintended and has no definable sender.

5. The Australian mathematician *Brendon McKay* used the method outlined in 'The Bible Code' on the English novel 'Moby Dick', and was able to similarly extract "sensational" predictions. *McKay* thus proved that the results of using this method are independent of the source used. One can find whatever one is looking for in a large enough supply of letters. Even fitting words of association can be discovered in the block of letters surrounding a find. And any words which do not fit (or which even contradict) the desired result are simply ignored by *Drosnin*. Incidentally, *McKay* found the word 'Drosnin' in the immediate vicinity of the word 'liar'.

Biblical Objections:
1. The central message of the Bible is the story of God's redemption of mankind, which culminates in the Gospel of Jesus Christ. Its purpose is to tell us who God is, who Jesus Christ is and to show us how we can be saved and attain eternity. The Bible does not concern itself with sensational political events. With his search, *Drosnin* sets himself against biblical revelation. The supposedly decoded messages in no way fit into the context of the Bible.

2. The words "discovered" by *Drosnin's* are put together arbitrarily, are not in any structured array, and do not form full sentences. The Bible expresses itself in comprehensible sentences, so that the meaning is easy to grasp (Eph 5:17). God has revealed himself in His Word (2 Tim 3:16; Gal 1-12; 2 Pet 1:21), and not in mysterious computer games. The message of the Bible is laid out so that even those new to faith can understand them (1 Pet 2:2). This message would not have been packaged in a secret code that could only be deciphered at the end of the 20th century.

3. *Drosnin* paints a distorted picture of God, which contradicts the Bible. For example, he writes: "The code seemed, instead, to be from someone good, but not all-powerful, who wanted to warn us of a terrible danger so we could prevent it ourselves" (p 103). In 'The Bible Code', the year 2006 (Hebrew year 5766) is connected with a comet, which destroys the earth (p 153). According to the Bible, the end of this earth will in no way be brought about by a comet, but by the Judgement of God (2 Pet 3:7,10). The Bible says that nobody can name the time for it, least of all 'The Bible Code'.

4. *Drosnin* writes: "But I don't know why I'm involved. I'm not religious. I don't even believe in God. I'm a total sceptic. There's no one who would be harder to persuade than me" (p 181). The Revelation of God, however, is only open to people who believe in Him and trust Him (Amos 3:7). Thus, *Drosnin* is a false prophet.

It is plain to see: 'The Bible Code' is, by its method, an arbitrary game of scrabble, which ignores basic aspects of information theory. This concept, based purely on the desire for controversy, allows room for irresponsible speculation. *Drosnin's* conclusions, fragments that are tacked together, contradict the nature of biblical revelation and thus oppose God and His Word.

3. Questions about Creation, Science and Faith (QC)

QC 1: *Can inanimate matter change into living organisms?*

AC 1: The historically sharp division between inorganic and organic chemistry was based on strong grounds: organic compounds were known to occur in nature only through the activity of living organisms. Once an organism dies, the process is reversed: the organic materials decay into their inorganic components. When, in 1828, the German chemist *F. Wöhler* (1800–1882) transformed the clearly inorganic ammonium cyanate into the organic compound urea (carbamide), this fundamental difference disappeared. One can synthesize numerous organic compounds nowadays through goal-oriented, planned effort. But to be able to do this, knowledge of chemistry and process engineering is required. In short, information is required. If we look at life forms we note that, at the physico-chemical level, there are no processes in plants, animals or people which contradict the physical and chemical processes operative outside of them. I.e., the known laws of nature fully apply here, too. Thus, in principle, there is no difference between inanimate matter and matter in living things in terms of physics and chemistry. Neo-Darwinian speculations on the origins of the first living things in a primordial atmosphere go even further in claiming a relatively smooth and uncomplicated transition from inanimate matter to living organisms. A living organism, however, should not be confused with the matter in living things. We will not have an adequate understanding of an organism by understanding its individual components in isolation. Organisms have one important ingredient, **information**, a mental quantity, which unaided matter is incapable of producing. Information is responsible for the fact that each living being develops to reach a particular final shape and is capable of reproduction. In inanimate nature, the principle of reproduction, i.e. on the basis of inherent information, does not exist. *Information thus becomes the characteristic trait in differentiating between a living organism and inanimate matter.* Similarly, the formation of an individual life form – in contrast to the formation of crystals – has nothing to do with a structure pre-determined by the demands of physico-chemical law. In the case of the phenomenon *life* we are dealing with a quality which goes beyond physics and chemistry. It is precisely those so-called evolution experiments, which are supposed to document the formation of life as a purely physical-chemical phenomenon, which validate our statement: *Information can never originate from a physical-chemical experiment!*

- During the frequently quoted *Miller* experiments some amino acids, the basic building blocks of proteins, could be synthesized; information was never produced. Thus, this attempt does not qualify as anything which could be called an evolution experiment.

- The hyper-cycle designed by *Manfred Eigen* (1927 –) is a purely mental hypothesis lacking any experimental confirmation. By using so-called 'evolution machines', *Eigen* wanted to bring evolution into the experimental realm. He said to the German journal 'Bild der Wissenschaft' (Issue 8, 1988, p 72): "In one of our machines we evolved bacterial viruses. … This project has already been successful. In a mere three days we could isolate a mutated form which showed the appropriate resistance. The example proves that it is possible to imitate the evolutionary process in the laboratory." Such statements give the impression that an evolution experiment was successful. In reality, the point of departure was an *already existing* life form. No new information was created. Instead, experiments are carried out on existing information, and consequently we are unable to say anything about the origins of information.

One important fact needs to be stressed: *no laboratory in the world has yet succeeded in* creating *living organisms from inanimate organic matter.* This is especially significant if one considers the many ways biotechnology has devised of manipulating living beings. Interestingly enough, biotechnology always starts off with a living being and merely tries to manipulate it. Clearly the gulf between chemo-technical processes and biotechnology seems unsurpassable. In fact, even if some day, after unrelenting research and the employment of all the knowledge in the world, this chasm should be crossed, it would only serve to prove that mind and creativity were required to create life.

QC 2: *How old are the earth and the universe? Is there a scientific method which can be used to determine the earth's age? What do you think of the carbon dating method?*

AC 2: As yet no physical method has been found to determine the age of the earth or of the universe. Why not? There is no clock in nature (in the form of a process recording time), which has been running since the creation of the world. At first sight, the radioactive decay of unstable atoms seems to be a possible clock. Every unstable isotope of a chemical element has its own half-life. This is the time period T in which the existing number of atoms is reduced to half by radioactive decay. Of the 320 isotopes existing in nature over 40 are known to be radioactive. This physical effect is the premise for radiometric age determination. One differentiates between the *long term clocks*

- uranium/thorium-lead clocks $T = 4.47 \times 10^9$ years for uranium-238 (^{238}U)

- potassium argon clock $T = 1.31 \times 10^9$ years for potassium-40 (^{40}K)

- rubidium strontium clock $T = 48.8 \times 10^9$ years for rubidium-87 (^{87}Rb)

- and the *short term clock* ^{14}C (in words C14) with $T = 5,730$ years.

For the mathematical treatment of equations of physical decay, however, there is always one unknown quantity too many. Such a system can never be solved mathematically. Physically this means: the initial amount of radio-active matter is unknown since nobody knows how many unstable atoms existed at the time of creation. Then there is the so-called 'isochrone method' which tries to get around having to know the initial amount by using congenetic samples only. The uncertainty shifts to the fact that there are no *a priori* criteria to ascertain whether a sample belongs to the congenetic entity.

The ^{14}C method (radioactive carbon decay) is a little different. Here the initial value can be ascertained by means of dendrochronology (counting of tree rings). Since the oldest trees are approximately 5,000 years old, each annual ring can be counted, giving its corresponding age. The oldest known plant still in existence is a bristlecone pine *(Pinus aristata)* in Nevada, which was 4,924 years old in 1998. Via the number of tree rings, we then have a calibration curve which now allows the age of a sample, whose age is unknown, to be determined by means of comparison. The carbon dating method can only be used for a few millenia, not for millions of years. The millions of years mentioned within the framework of the theory of evolution are not based on exact physical measurements but on the so-called *geological time scale* which assumes that the time period of each geological formation is proportional to its thickest layer found on earth. This theory presupposes that for all formations the maximum speed of deposition was always constant and always absolutely identical. Even from an evolutionist's point of view, this presumption is not tenable. How much less if one considers the flood as well.

Let us note: Physical variables (such as time) can be measured accurately only if a physical effect can be determined quantitatively during a process and this measured value can be recorded as a number of defined units with the help of a calibrating instrument (i.e. calibration curve or calibrated scale). If one submerges a mercury thermometer without temperature scale in hot water, then the mercury thread expands, but the actual temperature cannot be determined. A calibrated thermometer is needed for a control measurement and only this would give us the true value of the measurement. For the radiometric long term clocks there is no *calibrated instrument* (for example in the form of a natural process which records time periods).

The oldest *provable* secular history begins in the Near East and Egypt approximately 3000 BC. (It is interesting that this time span corresponds with the age of the oldest trees!). The Bible contains without doubt the oldest historical recordings. They go back to the first couple created by God. The consistent genealogical recordings supply us with the only ascertainable and reliable time frame since creation. Even if one concedes that the genealogies are not entirely unbroken, the result is an earth age of several thousands of years, but definitely not the millions of years which evolution assumes. The age of the earth, the universe and the beginning of mankind are the same, apart from the difference in days on which they were created.

QC 3: *How do distances of millions of light-years fit into your understanding of a young universe? Shouldn't we assume that* *the universe is at least as old as the time a light beam takes to reach us?*

AC 3: The statements made in the above question are correct in the light of our present understanding: at 300,000 km/s (the exact value, excluding zeroes after the decimal point, was defined at the '17th General Conference for Weights and Measures' in 1983 as 299,792,458 km/s) light has a very high but nevertheless finite propagation speed. Therefore each star we see *now* informs us not so much about its present existence, but its past, as the light beams which are reaching us now indicate. An (unauthorized!) conclusion is therefore: as there are stars which are several thousand millions of light-years away they must also be at least as many thousand millions of years old. To clarify this way of thinking, let us consider two important factors:

1. *Distance not time:* The light-year, like the metre, is not a unit of time but of distance. A light-year corresponds to a distance of 9.46 trillion kilometres. This is the distance light travels in one year. (Similarly, one can indicate the time light takes to travel one metre: 1/299,792,458 seconds. Incidentally, the former definition of the metre in wavelengths was replaced by the definition of light in time units.) If the distance between two objects A and B is known to be *a*, the knowledge of this distance does not of itself state anything about any other circumstance (e.g. age).

2. *Creation thinking:* The unhindered intellectual coupling of distance to time is a result of the evolution-orientated school of thought where both past and future have unlimited time at their disposal. According to Scripture, however, the time axis has a definite point of origin which is marked by the first verse in the Bible and which goes back several thousand, not millions of years. Extending the time axis past this point of origin is therefore physically impossible. To ignore this fact, would be like extending one's own existence past the point of conception. Let us go back and look at the week of creation from this point of view. On the fourth day the stars were created (Gen 1:14-16). According to the above train of thought not a single star would have shone in the skies when creation was completed. The star Alpha Centauri which is closest to earth, is 4.3 light-years away. It would not have been visible from earth until 4.3 years after its creation. The next star, Barnard's star (distance 5.9 light-years), would not have been visible until 1.6 years later. If that were the case we would still not be able to see all the stars today, since every year the light of a constantly increasing number of stars would reach us, depending on how far away they were from earth. However, this is contradicted by the observations of astronomers.

According to this school of thought, Adam would have looked up at a completely star-less night sky for 4.3 years. After another 1.6 years only two stars would have been visible. Abraham, who lived approximately 2,000 years after creation would not even have seen the brightest stars of the Milky Way, not to mention the stars of other galaxies, since the Milky Way extends over 130,000 light-years. But God showed Abraham the immeasurable *visible* number of stars in order to amaze him: "Look up at the heavens and count the stars – if indeed you can count them" (Gen 15:5).

The above concept of *number of light-years = minimum age of star* is therefore not scriptural. We find the biblical solution to this problem in Genesis 2:1-2: "Thus the heavens and the earth were *completed* in all their vast array [= *all* stars!]. By the seventh day God had finished the work he had been doing." The New Testament also testifies to this: "And yet his work *has been finished* since the *creation* of the world" (Hebr 4:3). As the week of creation came to an end, everything was perfected. This would include the stars since all of creation was *visible from the beginning* (Rom 1:20). It is part of the nature of creation that we cannot interpret all the laws of our present experience into the time span of creation. *Completed* means finished in every respect: the beam of light from the star was thus created just as the star itself; i.e. the light of even the furthest star had already *reached* earth. We need to remember: our scientific endeavours (thinking and research) will at best only lead us back to the end of the week of creation. To understand the events during the week of creation we need to study what the Bible says.

QC 4: *What did Darwin think of God?*

AC 4: After cutting short his studies in medicine, *Darwin* studied theology (1828 – 1831) on the recommendation of his father although his interests were in a different field. In his book 'On the Origin of Species by Means of Natural Selection' [Die Entstehung der Arten durch natürliche Zuchtwahl] he wrote: "There is probably something exhilarating about the belief that the Creator breathed the origins of life which surrounds us today into a few or even a single form only and that, while our earth moves in circles according to the laws of gravity, an infinite number of the most beautiful and marvellous forms was created from such humble beginnings." This formulation of *Darwin* merely shows a vague kind of deistic belief in God. God is acknowledged as the cause of the entire cosmic and biological development, but His personal position in relationship to man as well as to the biblical creation accounts are ignored. With the statement that man bears "the indelible stamps of his animalistic origin" *Darwin* clearly shows his broken relationship to the Bible. It was thanks to *Darwin* that the idea of evolution gained prominence and acceptance. He himself considered it to be an alternative to the biblical revelation, as he states in his autobiography: "At that time I slowly came to realize that the Old Testament because of its obviously incorrect history of the world ... was no more believable than today's books by the Hindus or the faith contents of the Barbars. ... Slowly I came to deny Christianity as divine revelation." This belief was strengthened in the following decades:

> "Disbelief slowly crept over me, and was finally complete. It went so slowly that it never troubled me, and ever since I have never even doubted for a second that my decision was right. Indeed I can hardly understand why anybody should wish Christianity to be true."

While *Darwin,* despite his complete denial of biblical revelation, still presumed a vague deism (i.e. regarded God as an impersonal being), *Ernst Haeckel* completed the step to total atheism by postulating "that the organism evolved by purely physical-chemical means." Today's Neo-Darwinists such as *M. Eigen, C. Bresch, S.J. Gould,* and *R. Dawkins* follow his thinking, and their reductionistic thoughts on the self-organisation of matter lead many to develop an atheistic or deistic, and thus anti-biblical world view.

QC 5: *In top competitive sports, performances previously thought impossible are bettered constantly. Doesn't this prove evolution?*

AC 5: On 3rd October 1988, in a concluding article on the 24th Olympic Games in Seoul, the daily newspaper in Brunswick *Braunschweiger Zeitung* stated:

> "The Games were given brilliance by 38 new world records. The limits of human capability were re-defined in the South Korean metropolis. Wretchedness is personified in the name of the dishonoured Canadian sprinter *Ben Johnson*, who ran his way to a world record and an Olympic victory

and was then revealed as a cheat. Only ten cases where performance had been illegally influenced were discovered by the IOC by Sunday. But the percentage of undetected drug abuse is far greater. Many top performances of Seoul are overshadowed by doubt. – The Games produced great athletes: the sixfold swimmer gold medalist *Kristin Otto* from Leipzig (Germany), the American swimmer *Matt Biondi*, decorated with 5 gold medals, the Russian 'gym king' and fourfold winner *Vladimir Artemow*, the American track-and-field athlete superstar *Florence Griffith-Joyner* with her sprint triumphs over 100 m, 200 m and in the relay. Without doubt *Steffi Graf* also belongs in the Hall of Olympic Fame for completing the 'Golden Slam' with her Olympic victory, thereby achieving a once-in-a-century performance."

Indeed, world records in top competitive sports are improved upon constantly. Even if one subtracts the cases of doping, an increase in performance is obvious. One thing, however, needs to be remembered: the records achieved are the result of intensive sports research and putting these findings into very taxing training methods. The top performances which were achieved through training are not hereditary. Once training is suspended, these achievements cannot be maintained.

In the system of evolution, however, a mechanism is required which results in unaided improvement from generation to generation. According to the theory of evolution, mutation and selection are the driving forces of evolutionary progress. But these are neither planned nor purposeful. On the contrary, a different law rules nature: the law of inertia, of passivity, of energy degradation and the tendency towards 'levelling off'. Life is always associated with purposefulness – even in the minute structure of the macromolecule. Nobody would doubt that today's computers are based on a complicated plan. But the architecture of even the most complex micro-processor circuitry is child's play when compared to the functions and systems in every living cell.

QC 6: *Can the Bible be taken seriously from a scientific point of view if it uses ancient concepts of the world which have long been outdated?*

AC 6: In no way does Scripture use the cosmologies of the time in which it was written. On the contrary: liberal theology interprets the concepts of the ancient Orient into biblical texts. *A. Läpple* writes from this standpoint, which sees the Bible as being of purely human origin:

> "The world was thought to be a round flat disc. It takes up centre stage of creation and is surrounded by *lower waters*, the first flood or the first ocean. … Above the earth's disc the firmament stretches like a shelter, to which sun, moon and stars have been fixed like lamps. Above the firmament are the *upper waters* which can stream towards earth through windows or sluices as rain" ('Die Bibel – heute', [The Bible today], Munich, p 42).

A couple of verses from the Bible suffice to deflate such an idea and to show how realistic the Scriptures were *before* the earth's shape – now proved to be spherical – was general knowledge:

In Job 26:7 we read: "He spreads out the northern {skies} over empty space; he suspends the earth over nothing." Earth neither floats on the first ocean nor is it fixed to a solid base; in fact it travels freely in the vacuum which surrounds it. The Bible also talks about the shape of the earth directly and indirectly, although imparting this information is not the primary purpose of the relevant passages: "He sits enthroned

above the circle {Hebr. *khug* = circle or ball} of the earth"
(Is 40:22).

The spherical shape of the earth is also clearly mentioned in
the texts relating to the return of Jesus. Since the Lord will
appear *suddenly* (Matt 24:27) and visibly for *all at the same
time* (Rev 1:7), it will be day for half of mankind when He appears, and for those living on the opposite side of the earth,
it will be night. This is what the text in Luke 17:34,36 touches
upon: "On that *night* two people will be in one bed; one will
be taken and the other left. Two men will be in the field;
one will be taken and the other left." The given situation of
simultaneous day and night on earth is characterized by the
work in the fields or resting in bed and depends only on the
position in which one finds oneself on the rotating earth at
that moment. Zechariah, too, testifies to the coming of the
Lord not in a way typical for the understanding of the world
in His times but realistically (Zech 14:7): "It will be a unique
day [= date], without the daytime or night-time [there will
be neither day nor night] – a day known to the Lord. When
evening comes, there will be light."

QC 7: *What can we say about the structure of our universe?*

AC 7: Man has tried with ever new hypotheses and models to
determine the structure of the universe based purely on the
theory of cosmic evolution. Among the "prophets of new cosmologies" as the German *Heckmann* calls them, we can name,
for example, *A. Friedmann, A. Einstein, E. A. Milne, P. Jordan,
F. Hoyle, G. Gamow, A.A. Penzias* and *R.W. Wilson*.

All scientific efforts to fathom the spatial structure of the
universe, open or closed, bounded or unbounded, finite
or infinite, three- or four-dimensional, convex or concave
have failed. The well-known astronomer *O. Heckmann*

says about these endeavours in his book 'Sterne, Kosmos, Weltmodelle' [Stars, Cosmos, World Models] p 129: "The inventiveness of the human mind is not small, therefore the production of world-views is rather great. As a result a critic recently believed that he was entitled to state that the number of cosmological theories is inversely proportional to the number of known facts." The German astrophysicist *V. Weidemann* from Kiel made an important observation in this context at the '16th World Congress for Philosophy in Düsseldorf (1978)':

"There are more philosophical assumptions on which cosmology is based than in all other branches of natural science. If, however, we are forced to retract the limits of what can be called science, and cannot hope to answer fundamental questions of cosmology scientifically, then we have to admit that the universe is basically incomprehensible. Science has to accept that there are questions which cannot be answered. What remains is a theory about what we know."

These findings are already recorded in the Bible. The key verse with regard to the unfathomability of the universe is found in Jeremiah 31:37: "'Only if the heavens *above* can be measured and the foundations of the earth *below* be searched out will I reject all the descendants of Israel because of all they have done,' declares the LORD." Here God correlates the results of astronomic research and the future of a nation – thus two totally independent circumstances are linked in one common statement. One portion is a promise of God's faithfulness toward Israel and the other is closely interlinked; no astronomic and geophysical research will succeed – despite greatest efforts – in comprehending the structure of the universe or the structure of the earth's core. Since God's promise to Israel is absolute and dependable, the same applies to the other statement: The astronomical and geophysical research goals mentioned can never be attained. Thus the goal of the paralysed British astrophysicist *Stephen W. Hawking* remains utopian: "We shall ... be able to take part in the discussion of the quest of why it is that we and the universe exist." The answer to this question, he writes, "would be the ultimate triumph of human reason" ('A Brief History of Time', Bantam Press, 1988, p 175).

QC 8: *How long was one day of creation?*

AC 8: Heated discussions have often ensued from this question, since so many contradictory theories have been developed, depending on one's point of view. We will arrive at an answer faster if we first clarify the number of information sources which could possibly be relevant. None of the current sciences has relevant empirical data available or facts to be interpreted. The only statements pertinent to the matter are made by God in Scripture, namely in the creation account (Gen 1) and in the Commandments of Sinai (Ex 20:11ff).

The creation account gives a tight chronology. All of creation was accomplished in six consecutive days. Once again the Bible proves itself to be an accurate book (comp. Principle 80 in the Appendix Part I) by using a physical unit in conjunction with the corresponding method of measurement (Gen 1:14). Thus, the length of one day – satisfying even scientific requirements – is defined. It is a geoastronomic time period which is determined by the time the earth takes to rotate, which is 24 hours. In the Ten Commandments given on Mount Sinai, God justifies the six working days and the day of rest for mankind with a reminder of the week of creation: "**Six days** you shall labour ..., but the seventh day is a Sabbath to the LORD your God. On it you shall not do any work ... for in **six days** the LORD made the heavens and the earth, the sea, and all that is in them, but he rested on the seventh day" (Ex 20:9-10).

In accordance with the theory of evolution the attempt is sometimes made to redefine the days of creation as long periods. The words from Psalm 90:4 "for a thousand years in your sight are like a day that has just gone by" are inserted into Genesis 1 arbitrarily as if they were a mathematical formula (in Psalm 90 and also in 2 Peter 3:8 we are talking about God, the Eternal One who is not subject to time). Such biblical mathematics supplies the desired time extension of 1:365,000 but it must be discarded as unbiblical. With the same justification this could be applied to Matthew 27:63, which would suddenly read: "after 3,000 years I will rise again." But Jesus rose again on the third day just as He had said. Critics have often objected that believing that God created the earth in six days is not crucial to salvation. I usually counter: Do you believe that Jesus rose again after 3 days? Normally the answer is yes. Then I conclude: Nor is it crucial to my salvation that the Lord rose after three days. But why differentiate in this way within the Bible? We believe one aspect, but distrust the other? Further arguments for the week of creation and objections against the arbitrary re-interpretation of the days of creation are dealt with in detail in [G2, pp. 13-55].

QC 9: *Are there two contradictory creation accounts?*

AC 9: The first two chapters of the Bible as well as numerous other scriptures deal with observations about creation. All accounts complement one another and, as a whole, describe in detail God's acts of creation. Underlying man's dealings with the Bible are two opposing basic general attitudes: one faithful to the Bible, the other critical of it. A person's decision in favour of one or the other attitude becomes apparent long before we start interpreting the resurrection of Jesus or His miracles in the NT. It begins in Genesis with two totally opposing kinds of scriptural understanding:

1. *Biblically faithful:* The creation account according to Genesis 1 and 2 (along with the rest of the Bible, which was written under divine inspiration, see 2 Tim 3:16) was not thought up by man. God Himself is the source of this information. No-one witnessed God's acts of creation and so He alone can tell us what happened by means of revelation. In stark contrast to this belief is the attitude described below:

2. *Biblically critical*: the creation account must be separated into the parts Genesis 1-2a and 2:4b-2:25 and accredited to different human authors, the elohist (young source) and the jahwist (older source) who came to different conclusions on the origins of the earth and life. After the Babylonian exile, individual pieces were combined into one. In this critical approach emphasis is placed on finding contradictions and differences in both accounts in order to support this two source hypothesis. The two main arguments are:

  a) the accounts differ because different names for God are used (elohim, jahweh)

  b) the texts differ in the order of creation:
      "plants – animals – man" in the first account and
      "man – plants – animals" in the second.

Important objections need to be made concerning these two pillars of the biblically critical hypothesis:

to a): God reveals Himself in the Bible as Father, Son and Holy Spirit with more than 700 different names (see also QG3) in order to tell us about His numerous character traits. Assigning different names for God to different authors – according to the above understanding it would be 700 at least – is an arbitrary assumption which does not correspond to the overall testimony of the Bible.

to b): Genesis 2:4b is not the description of a second creation account which stems from a different source. In these verses a certain detail is described at length, namely the creation of man. It is a parallel account to Genesis 1:2-3 with a different objective. The obvious emphasis is on *how, where and in which order did God create the first couple and what was their relationship with one another and hence with their Creator?* We find the same style of narration in other parts of the Bible. An event is first told in chronological order to create an overview and then, in a second account details are taken up and talked about at length. It is expressly said (v8) that God **planted** the Garden. The planting of a garden presupposes that plants were already created. After the planting "the LORD God made all kinds of trees **grow out of** the ground" (v9); this, too, should not be confused with the creation of the trees. Unlike the words used in Genesis 1, the words used here, namely "planted" and "grow out of" are not verbs of creation, since they describe actions which require the plants and trees to be in existence already. Furthermore, the interpretation of verse 19 is important: If one looks at this verse in isolation and deduces a theory from it (in breach of interpretation principle IP4, see Appendix Part II), one could presume that the animals were created *after* man. If one considers, however, that Genesis 2:7-25 is very anthropocentric (i.e. focusing on man), then it becomes clear that verse 19, too, does not deal with the actual time when the animals were created but that it tells us about the mental-vocal capabilities of recently created man: the naming of the animals by Adam. The next sentence is simply meant to indicate that the animals being brought to man were also formed by the Creator's hand – significantly enough, the *beasts of the field* are mentioned specifically and were also created on the sixth day of creation like man. To do justice to this background knowledge, we need to look at the Hebraic text of verse 19, which uses two tenses (bringing the animals and naming them is in the simple past tense, the 1st tense of the past; the forming of the animals in the past perfect, the 3rd tense of the past, here indicated by italics):

> "Now the LORD God *had formed out of the ground* all the beasts of the field and all the birds of the air. He brought them to the man to see what he would name them" (Gen 2:19).

QC 10: *Did the dinosaurs fit into the ark?*

AC 10: In the 40th chapter of the book of Job, dinosaurs are not only mentioned in passing, but actual details of their body structure are given (v15-18,23):

> "Look at the *behemoth*, which I made along with you and which feeds on grass like an ox. What strength he has in his loins, what power in the muscles of his belly! His tail sways like a cedar; the sinews of his thighs are close-knit. His bones are tubes of bronze, his limbs like rods of iron. When the river rages, he is not alarmed; he is secure, though the Jordan should surge against his mouth."

The NIV Bible does not translate the Hebrew animal name *behemoth* since no living creature in our day resembles the description of the above animal. The powerful tail could indicate a crocodile, but since it is carnivorous this does not correspond to the text. Another big animal which lives predominantly in water but also grazes, is the hippopotamus. It, too, is disqualified since it only has a small tufted tail. The only beasts which fit the above description exactly are the enormous animals belonging to the dinosaur group known as sauropods. The book of Job is counted among the oldest books of the Bible, but the exact time of writing is unknown. Because the earth's surface changed after the flood with totally different mountains, rivers, seas and oceans, the naming of the river Jordan in Job 40:23 is a clear indication that we are looking at the time after the flood, a time during which the dinosaurs were obviously still alive. These animals must therefore have also been saved by the ark. Grown animals would have taken up a fair amount of space in the enormous ark so that it is conceivable that Noah only took young animals or possibly just eggs. After the flood these animals no longer found the ecologic and climatic conditions which had previously been created for them, so as time went on they died out. This explanation for the extinction of the dinosaurs is more convincing than the hypotheses which are being thought up today in opposition to biblical assertions.

QC 11: *Whom did Adam's sons marry?*

AC 11: The first two humans, Adam and Eve, had two sons: Cain and Abel. Cain killed Abel and immediately following, we can read: "So Cain went out from the LORD's presence and lived in the land of Nod, east of Eden. Cain lay with his wife; and she became pregnant and gave birth to Enoch" (Gen 4:16-17). From where did Cain's wife suddenly appear?

If the Bible were to contain every detail which we can conclude for ourselves by rational thinking, it would have had to be a work of a hundred volumes. But God gave us only one book plus the gift of reason. Thus, we can answer questions that are not dealt with directly, but can be deduced from other statements.

We read in Genesis 5:3-4 that: "When Adam had lived 130 years, he had a son in his own likeness, in his own image; and he named him Seth. After Seth was born, Adam lived 800 years and had other sons and daughters." From this we can conclude that the first parents had many children. Therefore, Cain's wife had to be one of his sisters. The result of the Fall of Man was not only death and suffering but a gradually accumulating mutational degeneration of the originally perfect genes. By the time of Moses, about 2500 years after Creation, God forbade marriage between close relatives (Lev 18) because the mistakes occurring in the genetic material had accumulated to a level at which this would be harmful. However, at the time of Abraham, who lived 400 years before Moses, marriage between close relatives was still permitted, as we see in Abraham's marriage with his half-sister Sarah (Gen 20:12).

QC 12: *According to your understanding, which scientific arguments most favour creation and refute evolution?*

AC 12: Life confronts us in many shapes and sizes, but even a unicellular organism, despite its relative simplicity, is still more complex and purposefully arrayed than any man-made product. Two alternative, opposing principles are available for interpreting life and its origin: evolution or creation. According to the theory of evolution, life is defined as follows:

> "Life is a purely material occurrence, which must therefore be describable in physical and chemical terms, and differs from inanimate nature only in its complexity."

Numerous scientists from various fields (e.g. information science, biology, astronomy, paleontology, geology, medicine) have raised important objections to the theory of evolution. At the heart of the creation/evolution issue, however, an unresolvable controversy has persisted, due to the conflicting premises of the two models (see question QC 1). This stalemate could be avoided if there were an applicable system based entirely on empirical scientific principles. These would have to be formulated in such a way that they could be tangibly falsified by a single empirical example demonstrating the opposite. If no such example is found, they would gain the status of laws of nature and would thus have strong significance for the evaluation of unknown cases. In the same sense the energy premise, which has only been demonstrated by experience to be valid, can be applied independent of any worldview. Thus, the flight to the moon was possible only because the energy principle was assumed to be strictly valid. The **empirical principles of information** have the same status, so that we are now in a position to make, at the level of natural law, important deductions from these concerning creation/evolution.

Matter and *energy* are necessary basic qualities of living things, but they do not ultimately distinguish animate systems from the inanimate. The central and distinguishing characteristic of all living creatures is *information,* inherent in all life forms and necessary in every process (realization of all living functions, genetic information for reproduction). The transfer of Information plays a fundamental role in all living things. If, for example, insects transfer pollen from flowers, then this is primarily a transfer of information (genetic information); the matter involved here is secondary. This is not a conclusive definition of life, of course, but it is a crucial factor for our understanding.

Without doubt the most complex system which processes information is man. If one takes into account all of the information processes in the human body, i.e. *conscious* (language, information directing voluntary motor movements) and *unconscious* (organ functions, hormonal systems directed by information) then 10^{24} bits are processed daily. This astronomically large amount of information surpasses by a factor of one million the entire knowledge of mankind, which is 10^{18} bit, as stored in libraries around the world.

Looking at the question of the origin of life in the light of information theory, we need to consider the following empirical principles just as for any other system which transfers or processes information:

1. No information can exist without a code.
2. No code can exist without a free and deliberate convention.
3. No information can exist without a sender.
4. No information chain can exist without an intelligent origin.
5. No information can exist without an initial intelligent source, i.e. information is by its nature a *mental* and not a material quantity.
6. No information can exist without will.
7. No information can exist without the five hierarchical levels:
   - *statistics* (aspects of symbol frequency and signal transfer)
   - *syntax* (aspects of the code and sentence formation rules)
   - *semantics* (aspects of meaning)
   - *pragmatics* (aspects of actions)
   - *apobetics* (aspects of result and goal)
8. No information can originate by chance.

In the book "In the Beginning was Information" these principles are explained in more detail [G5, pp. 50-132]. Their status as Laws of Nature is justified [G5, pp. 26-49]. Thus the expression "Information Theory as Natural Law" is a fitting description.

In contrast to the theory of evolution life can therefore be defined as:

life = *material part (physical and chemical aspects)*
       + non-material part (information from mental source)

This short formula clearly shows that life has both a material and a non-material component. One aspect of the non-material is information from a mental source. But there is more to the non-material component of life. Straight after death, organisms still have genetic information in their cells. But something of fundamental importance is missing: that which means the difference between life and death. This difference is obvious to everybody, but it cannot be explained scientifically.

All concepts of an autonomous origin of information in matter (e.g. *Eigen's* hyper-cycle, *Küpper's* molecular darwinistic premise) have failed in practice. It is therefore a mystery to me that *Manfred Eigen* still believes that he will one day be able to explain the origin of information using purely material processes. "We must find an algorithm, a law of nature for the origin of information" ('Stufen zum Leben' [Steps toward life], Piper Verlag, 1987, p 41). His premise "information originates in non-information" (p 55) contradicts all empirical principles and is thus completely unrealistic. The above eight information principles, on the other hand, have proven correct in practice many times and have not been disproved in experiments carried out in any laboratory in the world. We should, therefore, ask ourselves whether life perhaps did originate in a goal-oriented creation process. This is the principle we find in the Bible. The mental source of information required by information science for any information – biological information included – is mentioned in the Bible on the first page: "In the beginning *God* created" (Gen 1:1). The theory of evolution, however, presupposes that the information in living beings does not require a sender. This argument is amply refuted by daily experience of the above laws of nature on information. This is why *information science today supplies us with the strongest arguments for the origins of life by creation*.

(W. Gitt: 'Information: The Third Fundamental Quantity', Siemens Review, Vol. 56, No. 6, 1989, pp. 2-7.

W. Gitt: 'Ist Information eine Eigenschaft der Materie?' West-deutscher Verlag, EuS 9, 1998, pp. 205-207.
W. Gitt: 'Laws of Nature about Information, one of the Basic Quantities Governing Biological Systems.' Pacific Symposium on Biocomputing, Kapalua, Maui (Hawaii), 4-9 January 1998; [G4, pp. 155-159).

4. Questions Concerning Salvation (QS)

QS 1: *We are saved by what – by faith or by works?*

AS 1: In the NT we find two statements which at first glance seem to be contradictory:

a) *Justification by faith:* "For we maintain that a man is justi-fied by faith apart from observing the law" (Rom 3:28).

b) *Justification by works:* "You see that a person is justified by what he does and not by faith alone" (James 2:24).

According to the central statements of the NT, believing in the Lord Jesus Christ saves (John 3:16; Mark 16:16; Acts 13:39; Acts 16:31). This saving faith is not simply the acceptance of biblical facts, but is a personal commitment to the Son of God: "He who has the Son has life" (1 John 5:12). Whoever turns to the Lord Jesus, experiences the biggest possible change in their life. This will be obvious in their way of life and their actions: "If you love me, you will obey what I com-mand" (John 14:15); "and you also must testify" (John 15:27); "put this money to work … until I come back" (Luke 19:13); "serving the Lord" (Rom 12:11); "love your enemies" (Matt 5:44); "do not repay anyone evil for evil" (Rom 12:17); "do not forget to entertain strangers" (Hebr 13:2); "and do not forget to do good and to share with others" (Hebr 13:16); "feed my sheep" (John 21:17). Ministry in the name of Jesus, using one's given talents, is an *indispensable result* of saving faith. In the NT these actions are called the *fruit* or the *deeds of faith*. Anyone who does not act accordingly, is thus damned: "And throw that worthless servant outside, into the darkness, where there will be weeping and gnashing of teeth" (Matt 25:30). Unlike the *acts of faith*, the *acts of the law* (Gal 2:16) or the *acts that lead to death* (Hebr 6:1; Hebr 9:14) are the acts of those who do not yet believe. Here, too, the same applies: if two people act the same way, it is not necessarily the same thing. The textual context of James 2:24 (see statement **b**) above) shows that the faith of Abraham resulted in concrete acts: he was obedient to God in leaving his homeland (Gen 1:21-6) and was willing to sacrifice his son Isaac (James 2:21). In the same way, the act of the (former) prostitute Rahab (James 2:25), namely saving the Israeli spies in Canaan, was a result of her faith in God (Jos 2:11). Thus, it becomes apparent: Faith and works are inseparably linked. Just as the human body is dead without its spirit, so faith is dead without acts (James 2:26). The above verses **a)** and **b)** are not contradictory but complementary (see Interpretation Principles IP3 and IP14 in Appendix, Part II).

QS 2: *Why did God devise the method of the cross for salvation? Was there no other way?*

AS 2: Crucifixion is not specifically mentioned in the OT. Having said that, some details are spoken of prophetically which can only refer to crucifixion, such as Psalm 22:16: "They have pierced my hands and my feet." Paul refers to the crucified Jesus (Gal 3:13) when he quotes the OT verse where it says "Anyone who is hung on a tree is under God's curse" (Deut 21:23). The Romans, who adopted this method of execution from the Persians, regarded it as the "most cruel, terrible" *(Cicero)* and "most dishonourable" method of all *(Tacitus)*. The cross was part of God's plan: Jesus "endured the cross, scorning its shame" (Hebr 12:2). He "became obedient to death – even death on a cross!" (Phil 2:8). Whether another method of death such as stoning, decapitating, poisoning, drowning would also have been conceivable, must be excluded by the analogy of Fall and salvation: through a *tree* (Gen 2:17: tree of knowledge) sin entered the world; it had to be eradicated on a *tree*. The cross of Calvary is the *tree of the curse* (Gal 3:13): Jesus dies, dishonoured and excluded from any human companionship: He is cursed.

The law of Moses puts a curse on the sinner. This curse has rested on all men since the Fall. Jesus accepted the Lord's curse on sin in our stead. The message of the cross is now the redeeming message for all of mankind who are cursed as a matter of course because of their sin.

Pope *John Paul II* once referred to Auschwitz as the Calvary of the 20th century. There is a theological school of thought today which sees Jesus in solidarity with the suffering of others, with the tortured and murdered who suffered as He did and died a gruesome death. But the death on the cross of Christ may never be compared with the death of other people, His cross may never be compared with the many other crosses which stood around Jerusalem or Rome. It has a different *quality* to the other crosses because it is the cross of the Christ, the Son of God. He suffered not only the injustice of the powerful of this world but was the **only one** who suffered the wrath of God over sin. He was the only sacrificial lamb who carried the judgment of God in the place of *many*. "The message of the cross" (1 Cor 1:18) has since been at the centre of all Christian preaching. Paul has therefore only one thing he wants to convey: "For I resolved to know nothing while I was with you except Jesus Christ and him crucified" (1 Cor 2:2). *Amelia M. Hull* shows us the meaning of the cross in a well-known revival song:

"There is life for a look at the Crucified One,
There is life at this moment for thee,
Men look, sinner, look unto Him and be saved,
Unto Him, who was nailed to the tree."

QS 3: *How could Jesus die 2000 years ago for sins which we are committing now?*

AS 3: God's salvation plan for fallen mankind existed even before the creation of the world (Eph 1:4). This was because God not only reckoned with the Fall as a result of the free will He gave but had already foreseen what would happen. God could have sent salvation through the Lord Jesus Christ immediately after the Fall or at the end of time; what is important is that it happened *at all* (Hebr 9:28). In the first instance the price for sin would have been paid in advance, in the second instance, it would have happened in retrospect. We are acquainted with both from the business world: payments in advance and in retrospect. God chose the optimum time in His wisdom. As we read in Galatians 4:4: "But when the time had fully come, God sent his Son." People who lived prior to Jesus and who listened to the teachings of God concerning salvation available *at that time* have been saved through the sacrifice on Calvary just as those who were born *afterwards* and accepted the gospel (Hebr 9:15). The time aspect of salvation is expressed in Romans 5:8: "But God demonstrates his own love for us in this: While we were still sinners, Christ died for us."

The laws did not exist during Abraham's or Job's time. These men acted according to their consciences and trusted God. This He credited to them as righteousness (Rom 4:3). During David's time, the laws of Sinai had been in existence for a long time. They were the standard against which God measured man. Sins were covered by animal sacrifices. The sacrificial animals could, however, not erase sin (Hebr 10:4). Animal sacrifices were simply a pointer towards the coming sacrifice of Jesus. This is why He is called the "*Lamb of God*, who takes away the sin of the world" (John 1:29). Only through Him can guilt be erased and the contrite offender be redeemed. We now live in the time when the sacrifice is complete and the symbolic image of animal sacrifice is a thing of the past. We receive forgiveness on the basis of the perfect and complete sacrifice of Jesus.

QS 4: *Wouldn't it have been sufficient for Jesus to only suffer for the sins for which man has asked forgiveness, instead of suffering for the sin of the whole world?*

AS 4: According to the Word of God, the wages of sin is death (Rom 6:23). Let's suppose that only one man during the entire human history had turned to Jesus because of the gospel, then for him the price of his sin would have been death. The author agrees with the thought expressed by *Hermann Bezzel* (1861–1917) that the love of Jesus was so immense that He would have died to save just one repentant sinner. The redeeming act of the Son of God, however, is of such magnitude that it is sufficient for all of mankind. This is why John the Baptist could say: "Look, the Lamb of God, who takes away the sin of the world" (John 1:29). Now everyone who wants to can accept that forgiveness. The following story illustrates this point:

A wealthy Irish landowner once gave a most ingenious sermon to the people tilling his lands. At all important points of his widespread landholdings he posted the following announcement:

> "Next Monday I will be in the office of my country residence from ten o'clock until midday. During that time, I will be prepared to pay all my labourers' debts. All unpaid bills should be brought along."

This unusual offer was the main topic of conversation for several days. Some thought it a malicious lie, others suspected a catch since nobody had ever made such an offer before.

Monday arrived and a number of people came to the stipu-
lated place. At ten o'clock exactly, the landowner arrived and
disappeared silently behind his office door. Nobody dared to
enter. The people started arguing about the validity of the
signature and the boss's motive. Finally, at half past eleven an
old couple arrived at the office. The old man, with a bunch of
bills in his hand, asked whether this was where the debts were
being paid. He was scorned: "Well, he hasn't paid anything
up to now!" Someone else said: "Nobody has tried yet, but if
he really will pay, then come out quickly and tell us." In spite
of the discouragement of their fellow-workers the old couple
went in. They were greeted cordially, the sums were added up
and they received a cheque signed by the landowner covering
the entire amount. They were still thanking him profusely
and heading for the door when the landowner said: "Please
stay here until twelve o'clock when I will close the office."
The two old people mentioned the crowd waiting outside to
hear from them whether the offer was meant in earnest. The
landowner remained adamant. "You took me at my word and
those waiting outside need to do the same if they want to have
their debts paid." The offer of the landowner was meant for
all his people, and his wealth was sufficient to cover all their
debts. However, only the couple that trusted his word had
their debts paid.

                    (Source: *Friedhelm König*, 'Du bist gemeint',
                              [I am calling you], p 127 ff abridged).

In the same way the death of Christ is sufficient for the redemption of the whole of humanity. "Consequently, just as
the result of *one* trespass [Adam's] was condemnation for *all*
men, so also the result of *one* [Jesus'] act of righteousness was
justification that brings life for *all* men" (Rom 5:18). The offer
of redemption is open to all and should be made known to
all. But only *those* who dare to trust the word of the Lord and
commit themselves to Him personally and completely will be
justified and saved.

QS 5: *Based on the sacrificial death of Jesus Christ, God of-fers all men redemption from sin. Why doesn't God just grant a general amnesty?*

AS 5: Because of Jesus' death on the cross God's offer of salvation is extended to all men. "In the past God overlooked such ignorance, but now he commands **all people everywhere** to repent" (Acts 17:30), this was the message of Paul on the Areopagus. Now nobody need perish because of their sin. Every sinner can be pardoned. If even Paul, who wanted to exterminate the church of Jesus, could be forgiven, how much more does this apply to everybody else. Of the two criminals crucified with the Lord Jesus only *one* was saved, the one who came to Jesus acknowledging his sinfulness. The other persisted in his rejec-tion and scorn of Jesus and so his sins were not taken away. This shows us that God does not grant a general amnesty but that He acts according to our individual decision:

> "I have set before you [eternal] life and [eternal] death, blessings and curses. Now choose [eternal] life, so that you and your children may live" (Deut 30:19).

> "This is what the Lord says: 'See, I am setting before you the way of [eternal] life and the way of [eternal] death'" (Jer 21:8).

Everyone truly seeking forgiveness will receive it irrespective of the seriousness of his guilt: "Though your sins are like scar-let, …" (Is 1:18). To drive the point home, we could say: a man is not condemned because of his sin, but because of his will, i.e. his unwillingness to repent. There will only be volunteers in heaven, no conscripts.

QS 6: *I believe salvation is possible after death. God's mercy must surely be bigger than what you have told us?*

AS 6: This question is asked often because it moves us deeply if we truly fear for the salvation of people who are (or were) close to us. In fact, a number of other questions arise: What about the people

- who have only heard about Jesus in diluted or distorted form?

- whose only contact with the Christian message has been the worldly-minded, often politically coloured sermons in their churches, and who then decided Christianity wasn't for them?

- who appeared to be Christian but whose innermost desires opposed the Bible?

- who apparently did not benefit from our evangelistic efforts because we did not touch their hearts or they did not want the gospel?

- who were brought up as atheists or in sects with false teachings?

- What about all today's young people who are influenced by the critical attitude to the Bible in Religious Instruction lessons at school and who therefore never think about faith again?

- And finally, what about those people who, through no fault of their own, never had the opportunity of coming under the influence of the gospel?

All of these questions have given rise to many different groups offering a host of answers, either suggesting salvation after death or rejecting damnation completely. We want to look at a few of these contradictory ideas below:

1. The *proponents of universal reconciliation* claim that after a period of limited punishment everybody will be saved: *Hitler* and *Stalin* as well as *Nihilists* and *Spiritists* (dealt with in more detail in [G3, pp. 106-108]).

2. According to Catholicism, the souls of the dead who still require purification go to purgatory before they are admitted into heaven. This belief was held in particular by *Augustine* and Pope *St. Gregory I, the Great*. The assumption that the pain of the 'poor souls' in purgatory can be shortened by the intercession of the living, gave rise to the letters of indulgence in the Middle Ages and the All Souls' Day in the Catholic calendar.

3. In the *Mormon Church* it is possible to be baptized on behalf of the deceased in order to save unbelievers even if they lived several generations ago.

4. The *Jehovah's Witnesses* believe that there is neither heaven nor hell for anyone except for the chosen 144,000. They believe their followers will inherit a new earth, and not enjoy eternal fellowship with God, the Father and His Son Jesus Christ in heaven. The others remain in the grave, or can be released through the so-called *ransom sacrifice*.

5. The *New-Apostolic Church* has instituted a death ministry according to which their self-appointed apostles can influence even the world of the dead. The gift of salvation achieved in this world is passed on to the deceased by the deceased apostles who continue their *salvation ministry* in the next world.

6. Other groups propose a belief whereby those who believe in Christ go to heaven and the unbelievers are wiped out entirely so that they no longer exist.

7. Another school of thought refers to the Scripture 1 Peter 3:18-20 from which some exegetes deduce that the gospel is preached in the kingdom of the dead with the objective of salvation (dealt with in more detail in [G3, pp. 146-153]).

All these schools of thought – I'm sure with good intentions – try to give hope to those groups mentioned initially. But these speculations do not help us any further so let us ask the only One who can provide us with an answer: God in His Word. Let us check with Scripture on whether there is a possibility of salvation after death. Since this is an extremely important question we can assume that God will not leave us in the dark about it (see cf Principle P51 in Appendix, Part II). Only the Bible can help us identify false teaching and keep us from being led astray.

1. Death is followed by judgment: In the light of the Bible, theories in which man is given another chance of finding salvation after death are revealed as flights of human fantasy because "… man is destined to die once, and after that to face judgment" (Hebr 9:27). This applies to people who have had contact with God's Word in one way or another as well as to those who have never heard it. "For we will all stand before God's judgment seat" (Rom 14:10). God has appointed the Son to be the judge. We will not be judged on what might still happen on the other side of death's door but on what we have done with our lives in the Here and Now "that each one may receive what is due to him for the things done while in the body, whether good or bad" (2 Cor 5:10). Nobody is exempt from appearing before the Judgment Seat of God: believers, those who are indifferent, atheists, freethinkers, those who are misled, pagans … in brief, everyone (Acts 17:31).

2. The criteria for judgment: The criteria for God's judgment are not arbitrary; nobody is given preferential or discriminatory treatment (1 Pet 1:17; Rom 2:11). God has given us standards and we will be judged only according to the rules revealed to us in the Bible: "that … word which I spoke will condemn him at the last day" (John 12:48). Let us list the most important criteria from Scripture:

a) *According to God's righteousness:* We may be certain: "It is unthinkable that God would do wrong" (Job 34:12) since He is a just judge (2 Tim 4:8). No distortions, no misrepresentations will exist since truth and justice will reign: "Yes, Lord God Almighty, true and just are your judgments" (Rev 16:7).

b) *According to what has been entrusted to us:* No person is exactly like another and everyone has been entrusted to a different extent. Those unreached by the gospel do not know as much about God. The only thing they know about Him is what they see in creation (Romans 1:20) and have implanted in their conscience (Rom 2:15). They know less than people who have had the chance to hear the gospel. A wealthy man has more opportunities to do good and help spread the gospel than a poor man. The intellectually gifted have special responsibilities. There is a difference between a person who lives under the limitations of a dictatorship and another who can act freely. The Lord says in Luke 12:48: "From everyone who has been given much, much will be demanded; and from the one who has been entrusted with much, much more will be asked."

c) *According to our works:* God knows everyone's actions and He "will give to each person according to what he has done" (Rom 2:6). Works are deeds that we have done (Matt 25:34-40) as well as those we omitted to do (Matt 25:41-46). Everyone's actions are written down in the books of the Lord and form the basis on which God will pronounce fair sentence during the judgment (Rev 20:12-13).

d) *According to our fruit:* Everything that we are and do in the name of the Lord (Luke 19:13) – our attitude, our conduct, our actions – is regarded by the Bible as eternal fruit (John 15:16). This fruit is a fundamental standard according to which we will be judged (Luke 19:16-27). While all dead works will be burned up (1 Cor 3:15), everything that remains will be rewarded (1 Cor 3:14) because it has eternal value.

e) *According to our love:* Love is a special fruit and it is the greatest of them all (1 Cor 13:13). It is the fulfilment of the law (Rom 13:10). This refers to that which we have done for the love of God (Matt 22:37) and for the love of Christ (John 21:15). Selfless love must be distinguished from calculating, cunning love: "If you love those who love you, what reward will you get?" (Matt 5:46). The Pharisee Simon invited Jesus into his home but he did not even give Him water to wash His feet as was the custom at the time (Luke 7:44). The sinful woman poured precious perfume over His feet. She received much forgiveness which is why she showered the Lord with love (Luke 7:47). Love is a fruit of the Spirit (Gal 5:22). It has eternal significance.

f) *According to our words:* According to Jesus what we say has implications for eternity. This aspect of judgment is perhaps the least known to us: "But I tell you that men will have to give account on the day of judgment for every careless word they have spoken. For by your words you will be acquitted, and by your words you will be condemned" (Matt 12:36-37).

g) *According to our responsibility:* Our created personalities are structured in such a way that responsibility is an inherent part of us. God has given us a lot of leeway for which we ourselves have to bear responsibility. Even when we are tempted, we are responsible for what we do. Although Adam's sin came about through temptation, he nonetheless had to bear the consequences of his disobedience. Since misguided belief ends in damnation, scriptural warnings concerning this are particularly emphatic (e.g. Matt 24:11-13; Eph 4:14; Eph 5:6; 2 Tim 2:16-18). For this reason, the false teachings of sects should not be underestimated.

h) *According to our attitude to Jesus Christ:* Our personal relationship with the Son of God is the most crucial: "Whoever believes in the Son has eternal life, but whoever rejects the Son will not see life, for God's wrath remains on him" (John 3:36). Sin brought damnation upon all men (Rom 5:18). The only way out is to cling to Christ: "Therefore, there is now no condemnation for those who are in Christ Jesus" (Rom 8:1).

3. The Judgement Sentence: Everyone will be judged according to the above criteria. No aspect of an individual's life will be overlooked. What is the final judgment? Mankind will be divided into two camps and Jesus invites us to choose in this life:

> "Enter through the narrow gate. For wide is the gate and broad is the road that leads to destruction, and many enter through it. But small is the gate and narrow the road that leads to life, and only a few find it" (Matt 7:13-14).

There is no *middle path* for those who cannot make up their minds and no neutral zone between heaven and hell. In the end only one distinction will be made between the saved and the lost. The Lord will say to the one group: "Come, you who are blessed by my Father; take your inheritance, the kingdom prepared for you since the creation of the world" (Matt 25:34), and to the others he will say: "I don't know you or where you come from … away from me, all you evildoers!" (Luke 13:25,27). Not only atheists and unbelievers will belong to the latter group but also people who knew about the gospel of Christ but did not respond positively to Him. They will cry in amazement: "We ate and drank with you, and you taught in our streets" (Luke 13:26).

4. Our response: After death, according to Scripture, there will be no more opportunities for salvation. The decision has to be made in this life, which is why the Lord Jesus says: "Make every effort to enter through the narrow door" (Luke 13:24). During the Judgment, all of God's books containing the details of our earthly lives will be opened (Rev 20:12). Blessed is he whose name appears in the Book of Life. The non-Christian religions do not stand a chance. We do not know how many of those people who never heard the Good News but yearned for God (Acts 17:27) and sought eternal life (Rom 2:7) will be saved. But for those of us who have heard the gospel, there will be no excuses and no escape (Hebr 2:3) if we ignore salvation. We will have had the chance of salvation. How this salvation can be obtained is explained in more detail in the Appendix (Part I, Point 10).

QS 7: *What about the children who died too young to ever have been able to make a decision? What about aborted babies and the mentally handicapped? Are they damned?*

AS 7: Before we answer this question we need to know when an embryo becomes a person. If we were to believe contemporary secular trends we might be led to believe that this depends on the arbitrary beliefs of individuals or state legislature. If we want to find a reliable answer to the important question as to when we become human beings – then we must look at the Bible. The individual creation of a human life starts with the union of the male sperm with the female egg. Every embryonic development requires the direct intervention of the Creator: "For you created my inmost being; you knit me together in my mother's womb. I praise you because I am fearfully and wonderfully made; your works are wonderful, I know that full well" (Ps 139:13-14). When God called Jeremiah He referred to the fact that He had already seen him as a leading figure and chosen him for this task:

"Before I formed you in the womb I knew you, before you were born I set you apart; I appointed you as a prophet to the nations" (Jer 1:5).

Let us note: Man is an individual from the very beginning and, according to numerous scriptures (e.g. Luke 16:19-31; Hebr 9:27), a creature made for eternity whose existence is never terminated.

But where does man go after he has crossed the valley of death? The issue is crystal clear for all those who have heard and accepted the gospel. The will of God is clear: "The Lord ... is patient with you, not wanting anyone to perish, but everyone to come to repentance" (2 Pet 3:9). Salvation or condemnation thus depend on our decision alone. We have the freedom of choice to be with God or to go to hell to be without Him. We can choose either path (Deut 30:19; Jer 21:8).

Children who die too young, aborted and mentally handicapped children, however, do not possess the ability to make such a far-reaching decision. According to false teachings in the Middle Ages, it was believed that the souls of non-baptised children would be damned if they died prematurely. This is based on the unbiblical teaching that baptism saves the souls of minors. According to the core teachings of the Bible, however, it is not baptism but faith in Jesus Christ which saves (Acts 16:31). Thus, the baptism of children (which in any event is impossible for aborted children) is of no help in answering the above question. We find the answer in the verse: "God Almighty ... is never unjust to anyone" ('Good News', Job 34:12) since His sentences are always just (Rev 16:7) and are carried out irrespective of person (1 Pet 1:17; Rom 2:11). So we can assume that the above-mentioned people will not be damned. They themselves are not to blame for their destiny. When toddlers (and probably infants as well) were brought to Jesus the disciples regarded this as a pointless disturbance for the Lord Jesus who had had an exhausting day. But Jesus took this opportunity to point out that children are special heirs of the kingdom of heaven: "Let the little children come to me, and do not hinder them, for the kingdom of God belongs to such as these" (Mark 10:14).

QS 8: *Was Judas not preordained to betray Jesus in order to make salvation possible?*

AS 8: One thing needs to be remembered: salvation was made possible not through Judas but through Jesus Christ. The death of the Lord Jesus was necessary, so that we might receive salvation. A man who was absolutely sinless had to bear the judgment on sin on behalf of the sinner. According to God's plan "He was delivered over to death for our sins and was raised to life for our justification" (Rom 4:25). From the point where Jesus declared this willingness, up until the actual crucifixion, a lot of people were involved, Jews as well as Romans: the Sanhedrin of Israel (Mark 14:64), the mob (John 19:7; Acts 13:28), Pilate, (Mark 15:15), and the Roman soldiers (Mark 15:24). Judas, too, was directly involved in the betrayal. There was no *divine compulsion*, it was his own voluntary decision. That the Lord Jesus knew the voluntary action of Judas in advance (John 13:21-30) and that it was prophesied in detail in the OT (Zech 11:12-13) is due to divine omniscience, not compulsion.

The motives of Judas are not clear-cut in Scripture. The founder of the seminary centre in Krelingen (Germany), *Heinrich Kemner* (1903–1993), even suggested that Judas wanted to force Jesus into such a crisis situation that He would finally have to demonstrate His power in Israel. According to this point of view, Judas could not imagine that Jesus would not act to prevent His death. Even though many people con-tributed directly to the death of Jesus, they were nevertheless not the actual cause, since Jesus died of His own free will for the sin of all men. Each and every one of us is involved in the death of Jesus since "he was pierced for *our* transgressions, he was crushed for *our* iniquities; the punishment that brought us peace was upon him, and by his wounds we are healed" (Is 53:5).

Peter disowned Jesus before an insignificant servant girl. This can be compared to the betrayal of Jesus by Judas. The basic difference between these two men (Peter and Judas) does not lie in their sin but in their attitude toward it. Since Peter regretted his denial (2 Cor 7:10 *godly sorrow*) and repented, he was forgiven. Judas, too, could have been forgiven if he had searched for this forgivness in the right place – at the feet of Jesus. But Judas did not return to his master, which is why the curse remained on him: "The Son of Man will go as it has been decreed, but woe to that man who betrays him" (Luke 22:22).

QS 9: *How can I bring a child into this world if the chances that it will perish as an unbeliever are 50: 50?* (Question put by a young woman who had just become a believer)

AS 9: Many couples do not want to bring children into the world in view of the population explosion, the increasing pollution or the imminent danger of war, given today's world-wide armament potential. The Federal Republic of Germany prior to re-unification had a negative birth rate, so that the population will have decreased by two million from 61 to 59 million at the end of the millennium. *Luther* expresses a different, more positive perspective when asked what he would do if the world were to end tomorrow: "I would plant an apple sapling."

The question asked initially reveals a great sense of responsibility. It shows that the young woman is aware of eternity and gives it priority above more superficial things. To clarify the matter, two separate questions need to be asked first: What does the Bible tell us about the number of children we should have and how does it answer the question concerning the salvation of our children? According to God's order of creation, we were created man and woman. The first command given by God to man was: "Be fruitful and increase in number" (Gen 1:28); this was never revoked. The capacity to conceive and bear children is a gift of God to humanity just as children themselves are. "Sons are a heritage from the LORD, children a reward from him" (Ps 127:3). To have many children is regarded as a special blessing: "Blessed is the man whose quiver is full of them" (Ps 127:5). "Your wife will be like a fruitful vine within your house; your sons will be like olive shoots round your table. Thus is the man blessed who fears the LORD" (Ps 128:3-4). God not only gives us children (Gen 33:5), it is also His great wish that we bring them up to love Him:

> "Fix these words of mine in your hearts and minds; … teach them to your children, talking about them when you sit at home and when you walk along the road, when you lie down and when you get up" (Deut 11:18-19).

If we obey God's advice our efforts will not be fruitless: "Train a child in the way he should go, and when he is old he will not turn from it" (Prov 22:6). We can therefore have children without hesitation, because if we bring them up in accordance with the above instructions, the likelihood that they will come to believe and be saved is great. The great promise of God applies here: "I love those who love me, and those who seek me find me" (Prov 8:17). God loves young people who turn to Him: "I remember the devotion of your youth, how as a bride you loved me and followed me through the desert, through a land not sown" (Jer 2:2).

As believers we can bring children into the world with confidence because the chance that they will perish is not 50:50 at all. God's promise surrounds them if we bring them up according to the Scriptures. The experience of many believing couples shows that their children also found the path of faith provided they were instructed in the ways of the Lord from an early age.

QS 10: *The Bible mentions God choosing man. Do we still have a free will if decisions concerning salvation and damnation were made long ago?*

AS 10: *Aurelius Augustine* (354 – 430) and *John Calvin* (1509 – 1564) in particular are the proponents of the so-called *predestination doctrine* (Lat. *praedestinatio*). It is a doctrine which presupposes divine predestination, meaning that men are chosen in advance for faith or disbelief, for salvation or condemnation. Because of the twofold possibility we talk about *double predestination*. We need to check this against what the Bible teaches.

In the answers to the foregoing questions we have highlighted the freedom of man in particular concerning his decision for or against a relationship with God. This could give rise to the impression that man alone acts and that God remains passively uninvolved. This does not correspond to what we find in the Bible. In Romans 9:16,18 we read: "It does not, therefore, depend on man's desire or effort, but on God's mercy. Therefore God has mercy on whom he wants to have mercy, and he hardens whom he wants to harden." Here emphasis is clearly on the action of God. Man is in the active and freely creative hand of the Creator just as clay is in the moulding hand of the potter: "But who are you, O man, to talk back to God? Shall what is formed say to him who formed it, 'Why did you make me like this?' Does not the potter have the right to make out of the same lump of clay some pottery for noble purposes and some for common use?" (Rom 9:20-21). Thus we have no right to salvation. The free decision by man always goes hand in hand with the free selection by God. The idea of selection is documented by the following Scriptures in particular:

- Matthew 22:14: "For many are invited, but few are *chosen.*"

- John 6:64-65: "Yet there are some of you who do not believe. For Jesus had known from the beginning which of them did not believe and who would betray him. He went on to say, 'This is why I told you that *no-one can come to me unless the Father has enabled him*'."

- Ephesians 1:4-5: "For he *chose* us in him before the creation of the world to be holy and blameless in his sight. In love he predestined us to be adopted as his sons."

- Romans 8:29-30: "For those God *foreknew* he also predestined to be conformed to the likeness of his Son, that he might be the firstborn among many brothers. And those he predestined, he also called; those he called, he also justified; those he justified, he also glorified."

- Acts 13:48: "When the Gentiles heard this, they were glad and honoured the word of the Lord; and *all who were appointed* for eternal life believed."

In order to understand Scripture with regard to election, it is of fundamental importance that we understand the following:

1. *Time:* Election takes place at a time which in any event is far earlier than our existence: Before the earth's foundations were laid (Eph 1:4), before creation (Jer 1:5) and from the beginning (2 Thess 2:13).

2. *Ministry:* Election is always concerned with serving God. Thus, God chose Solomon, for example, to build the temple (1 Chr 28:10), the tribe Levi to be priests (Deut 18:5); Jesus chose the disciples to be apostles (Luke 6:13; Acts 1:2). Paul was chosen to prepare for the ministry to the Gentiles (Acts 9:15) and all believers are chosen to bear fruit (John 15:16).

3. *Irrespective of person:* Election is not carried out according to human efforts or standards. Instead God looks at the insignificant: Israel is the smallest nation (Deut 7:7), Moses is no orator (Ex 4:10), Jeremiah considers himself far too young (Jer 1:6) and the church of Christ is regarded as unimportant in the eyes of the world (1 Cor 1:27-28).

4. *For salvation, but not for condemnation:* What does God intend – our salvation or our damnation? God clearly tells us His intention: "As a shepherd looks after his scattered flock when he is with them, so will I look after my sheep" (Ez 34:12). Jesus summarizes the reason for His coming into this world by saying: "The Son of Man came to save what was lost" (Matt 18:11). In Jesus, God Himself is looking to win men for eternal life in His presence. God's will for salvation is for all of mankind: "[God] wants *all* men to be saved and to come to a knowledge of the truth" (1 Tim 2:4). This will of God is also revealed in 1 Thessalonians 5:9: "For God did not appoint us to suffer wrath but to receive salvation through our Lord Jesus Christ." *One thing becomes clear*: There is a firm, indivisible link between *salvation* and *election*; but there is no such link between *condemnation* and *election*. God does not choose people to be condemned. Thus, God hardens Pharaoh's heart because of his stubborn attitude; in no way was this predestined from birth. There is a 'too late' as the Bible testifies time and again, but it does not teach predestination for hell. Herod could no longer hear after he executed John the Baptist; as a result Jesus no longer answered him (Luke 23:9).

Let us note: Both principles apply (they are complementary statements!). God chooses man for salvation. Man, however, is responsible for his choice either to accept or reject salvation. When the prodigal son decided: "I will set out and go back to my father" (Luke 15:18) the father ran to him to take him back (Luke 15:20). If we freely choose to accept salvation God's promise to us is fulfilled: "I have loved you with an everlasting love" (Jer 31:3) and "[I chose you] in him before the creation of the world" (Eph 1:4). Before we decide for God, he has already decided to be for us, long before we were born. God expects and respects our decision, but without His mercy no acceptance would be possible (Rom 9:16). Only God knows to what extent people are affected by His divine calling (Phil 2:13) and the exercising of their own free human will (Phil 2:12).

QS 11: *Can you prove scientifically that hell exists?* (Question put by a girl in Grammar School)

AS 11: Science is limited in its scope of assertions; this is often overlooked. Knowledge and explanations only stretch as far as processes in the material world can be measured. Where processes cannot be measured or expressed in numbers, science is unable to provide further answers. Thus, natural science should not exceed its given limits, otherwise it ceases to be a science and becomes pure speculation. Hence, science cannot offer any information about the origin or the end of the world. Nor can any science give us information about questions beyond death.

If science cannot tell us anything about the existence of hell, then there is one unique place where we can learn about it: On the cross of Calvary the realities of heaven and hell are exposed for us to see. The cross explains the meaning of the gospel best. If everyone were to get to heaven automatically the cross would be superfluous. If there were another religion or a different way to receive salvation, then God would not have let His Son bleed to death on the cross. The cross shows us clearly: hell and evil really do exist. Without Calvary, we would all perish (Rom 5:18). We can summarize the message of the cross as follows: here the Son of God saves from hell. Nothing greater has ever been done for man. The Lord Jesus preached vividly about love and mercy, grace and righteousness, and invitingly of heaven, but He spoke about hell with particular seriousness. He called hell a bottomless abyss, a place "where 'their worm does not die, and the fire is not quenched'" (Mark 9:48) and as a place of "eternal punishment" (Matt 25:46). In the light of this reality, He warns us even more intensely:

"If your right eye causes you to sin, gouge it out and throw it away. It is better for you to lose one part of your body than for your whole body to be thrown into hell" (Matt 5:29).

"It is better for you to enter life maimed or crippled than to have two hands or two feet and be thrown into eternal fire" (Matt 18:8).

5. Questions about Religions (QR)

The character of religions: Anybody can deduce from the works of creation that there has to be a Creator (Rom 1:19-21). Since the Fall, man's conscience has been aware of our separation from God and the guilt-ridden behaviour of man: "Since they [the Gentiles] show that the requirements of the law are written on their hearts, their consciences also bearing witness, and their thoughts now accusing, now even defending them" (Rom 2:15).

All nations have sought reconciliation with God using their *own* thoughts and wills and have developed the most diverse religions. The word religion stems from the Latin *religio* (= diligence, fear of God) which is most likely derived from the verb *re-ligiare* (to bind {back} to). This attempt to bind to God is basically attempted in two ways which characterize all religions: by means of rules devised by man (e.g. sacrificial rites) and by means of sacred objects (Buddha figurines, prayer wheels, the Kaaba in Mecca).

All human attempts to be reconciled to God I will call *religion*. The Gospel, however, is the exact opposite: God Himself acts and moves toward man. As a result, we do not call the biblical way a religion (dealt with in detail in [G3]).

QR 1: *There are so many religions. Surely they cannot all be wrong. Is it not arrogant to claim that the Christian faith is the only way to eternal life?*

AR 1: No religion saves. Not even 'Christianity' saves, if it is purely religion. There is only one God, namely the One who created heaven and earth. Our only source of information on this God is the Bible. Only He can truly tell us how we can be saved. If there were any religion capable of saving us from being lost for eternity, God would have made this known to us. Jesus' death on the cross would then not have been necessary. Since the sacrifice of Calvary did take place, it must be absolutely vital for salvation. The cross of Jesus clearly indicates that there was no less costly method to wipe out our sin before the holy God. God judged our sin in Jesus' death on the cross. As a result, only turning to Jesus Christ and surrendering your life to Him can save. Religion requires that man tries to save himself by his own efforts; according to the gospel, God accomplished everything through His own Son and man only needs to receive salvation through faith. That is why Acts 4:12 states so categorically: "Salvation is found in *no-one else*, for there is no other name under heaven given to men by which we must be saved." There is no other bridge to heaven besides Jesus.

All religions are just shimmering mirages in the wasteland of lost mankind. A man dying of thirst is not saved by the mirage of a spring. In the same way, being tolerant towards all these man-made fantasies leads men to destruction (Prov 14:12). Man needs fresh water. The Bible clearly testifies to the only real oasis, the only chance of survival, Jesus Christ:

> "I am the way and the truth and the life. No-one comes to the Father except through me" (John 14:6).

> "For no-one can lay any foundation other than the one already laid, which is Jesus Christ" (1 Cor 3:11).

> "He who has the Son has life; he who does not have the Son of God does not have life" (1 John 5:12).

QR 2: *Do we not all, i.e. Christians and Muslims, pray to the same God?* (Question put by a Muslim)

AR 2: "May I counter with another question: Is your God Allah the Father of Jesus Christ?" – "No, Allah has no son. That would be blasphemy!" – "You see, then your God and my God cannot be one and the same." In view of the many religions, lots of people wonder whether they do not all worship the same God. Even in Old Testament times, the God of the Bible testifies to being "the first and ... the last; apart from me there is no God" (Is 44:6). "I, even I, am the LORD, and apart from me there is no saviour" (Is 43:11). This living God is the God of Abraham, Isaac and Jacob (Matt 22:32), He is the Father of Jesus Christ (Mark 14:36). Listed below are differences between Allah and the Father of Jesus Christ which must be mentioned:

1. *The relationship between God and man:* In the Islamic faith, God does not reveal Himself at all. He remains at a distance. The constant call "Allahu akbar" – God is still the greatest – manifests: One cannot enter into a relationship with Allah – he always remains in the other world, like an oriental ruler enthroned high above his subjects.

2. *Father – child relationship:* For a Muslim, the concepts of men being God's children and God being a Father (Abba, dear Father; Rom 8:15) are not only incomprehensible but blasphemous, since Allah lives strictly apart from this world.

3. *God as man:* The crucial event in the Bible's salvation account is God becoming man in Jesus Christ. God not only walked among us, He suffered for the sins of the world on the cross. The resultant salvation of man is inconceivable to the Muslim.

4. *God's mercy and love:* God is merciful to the sinner and the price paid for His mercy is unbelievably high: "You have burdened me with your sins and wearied me with your offences" (Is 43:24). God is merciful to us because our salvation cost Him dearly (1 Cor 6:20; 1 Pet 1:19). The mercy of Allah cost him nothing.

5. *God is our confidence:* The Islamic faith cannot conceive of a God who gives us peace and assurance of salvation: "For I am convinced that neither death nor life ... will be able to separate us from the love of God that is in Christ Jesus our Lord" (Rom 8:38-39). The Islamic faith cannot conceive of God humbling Himself on the cross and the Holy Spirit being poured out in our hearts. It cannot imagine Jesus' Coming in glory.

The God of the Qur'an and the God of the Bible may show verbal similarities here and there. But on closer inspection they do not have much in common. Therefore it is not the same God to whom Christians and Muslims pray.

QR 3: *How can I find out whether the gospel is of divine origin and not religion?*

AR 3: A few marked differences between religions and the gospel can help us here in our search for the truth:

1. In all religions, man initiates the search for God but no one who has undergone this search can truly claim: I have found a personal relationship with God; I have peace in my heart; my sins are forgiven; I have the assurance of eternal life. In the gospel of Jesus Christ, God approaches us. He bridges the chasm of sin with the cross and gives us salvation. Everyone who accepts this can testify: "For I am convinced that neither death nor life ... will be able to separate us from the love of God" (Rom 8:38-39).

2. The prophetic announcements pertaining to the Saviour in the OT (e.g. Gen 3:15; Num 24:17; Is 11:1-2; Is 7:14) have been fulfilled literally. In no other religion do we find prophecies that are not only spoken but also fulfilled.

3. God has condemned all religions as idolatry and sorcery (1

Cor 6:9-10; Gal 5:19-21; Rev 21:8). None of the many religions has saving character (Gal 5:19-21). If there was such a religion which could save, then Jesus would have commended it to us, and would not have had to die the bitter death of the cross. But the Son of God went to the cross, in order to accomplish the only possibility of our salvation. Which is why He says, "Therefore go and make disciples of all nations!" (Matt 28:19).

4. God affirmed the sacrifice of Jesus Christ in His resurrection from the dead (Rom 4:24-25). It is the only empty tomb in world history: "Why do you look for the living among the dead? He is not here; he has risen!" (Luke 24:5-6). All the founders of religions have died and remained dead.

5. In all religions man attempts to redeem himself through his actions. The gospel, in contrast, is the act of God. We cannot contribute anything to the act of redemption on Calvary: we were bought at a price (1 Cor 6:20).

6. Religions are based on a false idea of mankind and paint an equally false picture of God. Only the Bible can truly tell us who we are and who God is. On our own we cannot change ourselves in a way that would please God "for all ... fall short of the glory of God" (Rom 3:23).

7. In no religion does God leave heaven to redeem man. In Jesus, God became man: "The Word became flesh and lived for a while among us. We have seen his glory, the glory of the one and only, who came from the Father, full of grace and truth" (John 1:14).

Jesus Christ is therefore not an alternative to religion. He is the denial and rejection of it. He is the only way home – to the Father's home (John 14:6).

6. Questions on Life and Faith (QL)

QL 1: *Why are we here?*

AL 1: Our existence cannot be put down to an evolutionary process. The reason for our existance is because it was God's will to create man. Nowhere in the Bible do we read the reason for the creation of man, for example because God was lonely, because He enjoyed creating, because He wanted a partner or because He wanted to create beings He could love. In Genesis 1:26-27 God's decision to create man and how He did this is recounted: "Then God said, 'Let us make man in our image, in our likeness'. So God created man in his own image, in the image of God he created him; male and female he created them." This shows clearly that our creation was the will of God. We are neither "cosmic loiterers" *(Friedrich Nietzsche; 1844 – 1900)* nor "gypsies at the edge of the universe" *(Jaques Monod; 1910–1976)* nor climbers from the animal kingdom, but we originate from a specific creative act of God.

Furthermore, the Bible tells us that God loves us: "I have loved you with an everlasting love; I have drawn you with lovingkindness" (Jer 31:3) or "For God so loved the world that he gave his one and only Son, that whoever believes in him shall not perish but have eternal life" (John 3:16). This verse also tells us that we were made to have eternal life.

QL 2: *What is the purpose of life?*

AL 2: Man is the only earthly creature searching for a purpose in life. Three basic questions trouble us: Where do I come from? What purpose does my life have? Where am I going? Many have considered these questions. The German philosopher *Hans Lenk* from Karlsruhe emphasizes that we need not expect any answers from his specialized field, when he writes: "Philosophy hardly ever gives final solutions with regard to content. It is a subject concerning problems, not matter and solution. Philosophy sometimes considers a new problem perspective far more important than a partial solution to a given question." The poet *Hermann Hesse* (1877–1962) wrote: "Life is senseless, cruel, stupid and yet marvellous – it does not mock man, but it does not care more about man than about an earthworm." The French existentialist writer and atheist *Simone de Bouvoir* (1908–1986) loses herself in senselessness: "What purpose does life have if it is radically destroyed, nullified? Why did it exist in the first place? In the end, everything is senseless: the beauty of life, the deeds of men, everything. Life is absurd." Sciences such as psychology, biology, or medicine cannot give us answers either, since the question of life's purpose does not belong to their field of expertise.

Some people see the purpose of their life in

- *doing good:* Many nurse this humanitarian idea which is not specifically Christian. Christians are indeed commanded to do good (Gal 6:10; 2 Thess 3:13) but good deeds alone do not make a Christian.

- *achieving acclaim and honour:* Athletes strive for world titles and gold medals. Artists search for recognition on the stages of this world.

- *creating something immortal.* In this way people believe they can live on through their children or in society (e.g. foundations to which their names are linked). Others wish to immortalize themselves in their own poems, memoirs, diaries or the like.

We should remember: all worldly acclaim and honour are transitory. It is of no use to us after we die because where we will be going we "never again will have a part in anything that happens under the sun" (Eccl 9:6).

If our life is God's creation then it can be purposeful only if it is lived in harmony and communion with God and guided by Him. Man's heart – even if it possessed all the pleasures and delights of this world – would remain restless, empty and unfulfilled if it did not find rest and peace in the Lord. So we need to find out what God says the purpose of our lives is. Three points can clarify this:

1. God's goal for our lives is that we come to faith in Him. Without redeeming faith in the Lord Jesus Christ, we would be lost forever. This is why Paul said to the jailer in Philippi: "Believe in the Lord Jesus, and you will be saved – you and your household" (Acts 16:31). God wants "all men to be saved and to come to a knowledge of the truth" (1 Tim 2:4). Since this salvation is the most important thing in everyone's life, the Lord Jesus said to the paralytic who was brought to Him by his friends: "Your sins are forgiven!" (Matt 9:2). The salvation of the soul has priority in the eyes of God before physical healing.

2. Once we are saved, we are in the service of God: "Serve the LORD with gladness" (*King James Version*, Ps 100:2). As followers of Christ our life should be geared toward making disciples (Matt 28:19).

3. "Love your neighbour as yourself" (Matt 22:39). With this command to love, God places a burden on us not only for those far away on other continents, but foremost for those who have been entrusted to us: our spouse, our children, our parents, our neighbours, our colleagues. The Bible takes it for granted that we love ourselves, but this love should also be shared with our neighbours.

Points 2 and 3, serving the Lord and loving our neighbour, are what the Bible calls the fruit in our lives. Contrary to all transitory success, only this fruit is immortal (John 15:16). God will look for this fruit at the end of our lives and will ask us what we did with the pounds entrusted to us (life, time, money, gifts) (Luke 19:11-27). Even the glass of cold water which we gave in the name of Jesus suddenly assumes eternal importance (Matt 10:42).

QL 3: *How can I reconcile daily life and faith?*

AL 3: There will be obvious changes in the life of anyone who believes in Jesus wholeheartedly. Three characteristics mark the new way of life:

1. Break with sin: Conversion includes the forgiveness of our sins. We now live differently since sin no longer has any hold on us. As born-again Christians we are not without sin, but what was previously normal and everyday, now assumes the proportions of a train disaster. Observing the commandments, which were not given as prohibitions but as guidelines for a successful life, will change the course of our lives. This new orientation shows God that we love Him (1 John 5:3). To our fellowmen we are "a letter from Christ" (2 Cor 3:3) which can be read by everyone.

2. Faith in our daily lives: Everyone who believes in Christ and hence diligently reads the Bible, will find a wealth of helpful scriptures for all areas of life. A selection will be given below. Since this section deals almost exclusively with the practical aspects of faith, the OT books of Proverbs and Ecclesiastes are quoted frequently. We find advice concerning our own person (2a) and the interaction with others (2b).

2a) *Our person:*
- body (Rom 13:14; 1 Cor 3:17; 1 Cor 6:19)
- eating and drinking (Prov 23:20)
- kind of food prior to the Fall (Gen 1:29)
- kind of food after the flood (Gen 9:3-4; 1 Cor 8:8; Col 2:16; 1 Tim 4:3-5)
- sleep (Ps 4:9; Prov 6:6-11; Prov 20:13; Eccl 5:12)
- necessary work (Ex 20:9-11; Ex 23:23; Prov 6:6-11; Prov 14:23; Prov 18:9; Prov 21:25; Eccl 3:13; Eccl 10:18; 2 Thess 3:10)
- work as a principle of life (Eccl 2:3-11)
- remuneration of workers (Is 65:23; Jer 22:13; Luke 10:7)
- leisure time (Prov 12:11b)
- acquiring money and possessions (Eccl 4:6; 1 Tim 6:6-8; Hebr 13:5)
- worldly desires, worldly values (Eccl 2:2-11)
- possessions (Matt 6:19; Prov 10:22)
- wealth (Prov 11:28; Prov 13:7; Prov 14:24; Eccl 5:19)
- building a house (Ps 127:1; Jer 22:13)
- sport (1 Cor 9:24-25; 1 Tim 4:8)
- worries (Ps 55:22; Prov 12:25; Phil 4:6; 2 Tim 2:4; 1 Pet 5:7)
- marital sex (Prov 5:18-19; Eccl 9:9; 1 Cor 7:3-6)
- extramarital sex (Prov 5:20-23; Prov 6:24-32; Jer 5:8-9; Hebr 13:4b)
- sin (Gen 4:7; Ps 65:3; Lament 3:39; John 20:23; 1 John 1:9; 1 John 5:17; Hebr 12:1)
- alcohol (Ps 104:15; Prov 23:29-35; Prov 20:1; Eph 5:18; 1 Tim 5:23)
- language (Ps 119:172; Prov 12:14,22; Prov 14:3,5; Prov 18:20-21; Prov 25:11; Eph 5:19; Col 4:6; James 1:19; Hebr 13:15)
- temptation (1 Pet 1:6-7; James 1:2,12)
- accusing conscience (1 John 3:20)
- wrath (Eph 4:26)
- time (Luke 19:13b; 1 Cor 7:29; Eph 5:16)

- attitude (Phil 2:5)
- dreams (Eccl 5:3,7)
- happiness and joy (Ps 118:24; Prov 15:13; Prov 17:22; Phil 4:4; 1 Thess 5:16)
- doing good for oneself (Matt 22:39)
- accurate weights (Prov 11:1,24; Prov 20:10)
- personal philosophy or religion (Prov 14:12)
- youth (Ps 119:9; Eccl 11:9; Eccl 12:1)
- age (Ps 71:9)
- death (Job 14:5; Ps 88:4; Eccl 8:8)

What to do in:
- illness (Eccl 7:14; James 5:14,16)
- trouble (Ps 46:2; Ps 50:15; Ps 77:3; Ps 73:21-28; Ps 107:6-8; Phil 4:19)
- depression (Ps 42:5; Ps 119:25)
- fear of men (Ps 56:1-2; Ps 118: 6,8; Prov 29:25)
- disaster (Is 45:7, Lament 3:31-37; Amos 3:6)
- daily activities (Eccl 9:10; Col 3:17)
- giving (Prov 11:24-25; Eccl 11:1; Mal 3:10; 2 Cor 9:6-7)
- putting up security (Prov 6:1-3; Prov 11:15; Prov 17:18)
- taking a deposit (Ex 22:25-26)
- searching for guidance (Ps 37:5; Ps 86:11; Ps 119:105)
- searching for a spouse (Songs 3:1; Amos 3:3; 2 Cor 6:14)
- suffering because of righteousness (1 Pet 3:14)
- false teachings (Col 2:8; 2 Pet 3:17; 1 John 4:6)
- making plans (Eccl 9:10; Phil 4:13; Col 3:23)

2b) *interaction with others:*
- spouse (Eph 5:22-28; 1 Pet 3:1-7; Hebr 13:4)
- children (Deut 6:7; Prov 13:1; Eph 6:4; Col 3:21; 1 Tim 3:12)
- parents (Ex 20:12; Prov 6:20; Prov 30:17; Eph 6:1-3)
- friends (Micah 7:5)
- god-fearing and virtuous wife (Prov 12:4a; Prov 31:10-31)

- shrewish and undisciplined wife (Prov 11:22; Prov 12:4b; Prov 21:19)
- enemies (Prov 25:21-22; Matt 5:22,44; Rom 12:14)
- evil men (Prov 1:10; Prov 24:1-2; 1 Pet 3:9)
- fools, simple-minded people (Prov 9:8; Prov 23:9)
- believers (Rom 12:10; Gal 6:2,10b; Eph 4:32; Phil 2:4; 1 Pet 3:8-9)
- unbelievers (Matt 10:32-33; Acts 1:8; Col 4:5; 1 Pet 2:12,15)
- advisors (Prov 15:22)
- fellow men (Matt 22:39; Gal 6:10a; 1 John 4:20-21)
- spiritual teachers (Hebr 13:7)
- the sick (Matt 25:36; James 5:14-16)
- doctors and medicine (Matt 9:12; 1 Tim 5:23)
- strangers and guests (Matt 25:35; Rom 12:13; Hebr 13:2)
- the poor (Prov 3:27; Prov 19:17; Matt 25:34-40)
- the sidetracked (James 5:19)
- false prophets (1 John 4:1-3; Jude 18-19)
- doubters (Jude 22-23)
- widows (1 Tim 5:3; James 1:27)
- happy people or those in mourning (Prov 17:22; Rom 12:15)
- the aged (Lev 19:32; Prov 23:22; 1 Tim 5:1)
- the deceased (Eccl 9:5-6)

2c) *tips for dealing with:*
- the congregation (Acts 2:42; Hebr 10:25)
- creation (Gen 1:28)
- the government (Matt 22:21; Rom 13:1-7; 1 Pet 2:13)
- Israel (Zech 2:12)

3. In the world, not of the world: The Lord Jesus condensed the framework of His disciples' actions as follows: "You *do not belong to the world*, but I have chosen you out of the world. That is why the world hates you" (John 15:19). Whoever believes in Jesus, still lives in this world like everybody else but

in addition to what is mentioned under point 2, his attitude to
life has an eternal dimension. This eternal dimension affects
the believers' relationship with God, the Father and His Son,
as well as his attitude.

3a) *Our relationship with God and Jesus Christ. We are to:*
- love **God** (Deut 6:5; Ps 31:24; Matt 22:37)
- get to know Him (Ps 46:10)
- believe in Him (Hebr 11:6)
- think about Him (Prov 3:5-6; Eccl 12:1)
- keep His commandments (Eccl 12:13; Micah 6:8)
- thank Him (Ps 107:8; Eph 5:20; Col 4:2)
- praise Him (Ps 103:1-2; Eph 5:19b)
- sing to Him (Ps 68:4; Ps 96:1)
- call to Him (Ps 50:15)
- worship Him (Matt 4:10b)
- draw close to Him (James 4:8)
- love the Lord **Jesus** (John 21:16; 2 Cor 5:9; 2 Tim 4:8)
- call to Him (Acts 7:59; Rom 10:13)
- praise Him (Rev 5:12)
- accept Him (John 1:12)
- believe in Him (Mark 16:16; John 11:25-26; Acts 16:31;
  1 John 3:23)
- get to know Him better (Eph 4:13)
- obey Him (2 Cor 10:5; 1 Pet 1:22)
- follow Him (Luke 14:27; Luke 14:33)
- serve Him (Eph 6:7)
- have communion with Him (John 15:2; 1 Cor 1:9;
  1 Cor 11:23-29; 1 John 1:3)
- remain in Him (John 15:4)
- pray to Him and in His name (John 14:13-14; Acts
  7:58; Eph 5:20)

3b) *Spiritual activities and attitudes:*
- give the Lord's kingdom highest priority (Matt 6:33;
  Col 3:2)

- bring forth fruit (Luke 19:13)
- bring forth fruit of the Spirit (Gal 5:22; Eph 5:9)
- collect treasures in Heaven (Matt 6:20)
- spread God's Word (2 Cor 5:20; 1 Thess 1:8)
- do what pleases God (Eph 5:10; 1 Thess 2:4)
- spread the Gospel (Matt 28:19-20; Phil 1:27; 1 Tim 6:12)
- cultivate fellowship with believers (Matt 18:20; Acts 2:42)
- live pure and undefiled lives (1 Thess 4:3; 2 Thess 2:13; Hebr 12:14)
- read the Bible frequently (Jos 1:8; Ps 119:162; Col 3:16)
- have spiritual goals (Ps 39:4; Phil 3:14)

QL 4: *I have constantly recurring dreams which trouble me. How should I interpret these dreams?*

AL 4: There are three different types of dreams:

1. *Dreams from God:* The Bible mentions several dreams through which God spoke to certain men (e.g. Joseph: Matt 1:19-25). Either the dreamer recognized God as the immediate communicator (e.g. Solomon: 1 Kings 3:5-15; Daniel: Daniel 7) or God sent someone to interpret His message (e.g. Joseph interpreted the dreams of the baker and the cupbearer). Dreams in which God speaks to us can be recognized by the fact that even if they burden or frighten us, they soon prove to be of specific help to us in our daily life. However, experience has shown that God uses dreams to speak to us only on rare occasions.

2. *Meaningless dreams:* Most dreams are transient and meaningless as is stated in Job 20:8: "Like a dream he [the glory of the wicked] flies away, no more to be found, banished like a vision of the night." The current practice of symbolic dream interpretations should be rejected. "The idols speak deceit.

Diviners see visions that lie" (Zech 10:2). In the apocryphal book of Sirach (Ecclesiasticus) 34:1-8 we also find a helpful explanation:

> "Vain hopes delude the senseless, and dreams give wings to a fool's fancy. It is like clutching a shadow, or chasing the wind, to take notice of dreams. What you see in a dream is nothing but a reflection, like the image of a face in a mirror. Purity cannot come out of filth; how then can truth issue from falsehood? Divination, omens, and dreams are all futile, mere fantasies, like those of a woman in labour. Unless they are sent by intervention from the Most High, pay no attention to them. Dreams have led many astray and ruined those who built their hopes on them. Such delusions can add nothing to the completeness of the law; the wisdom spoken by the faithful is complete in itself."

3. *Dreams of events which have not been fully overcome:* Dreams can originate in the unconscious, which eludes the conscious will and mind. The cause of the dreams is obvious: unconquered fears, unconfessed guilt, events that have not been overcome yet (e.g. war memories, exam fears, marital crises). This is probably the type of dream mentioned in the question. Extended counselling will help the healing process. Since guilt always causes problems, we need to forgive and be forgiven.

QL 5: *What is sin?*

AL 5: Before the Bible talks about *sin* it illustrates how it came into being (Gen 3:1-13). It does not state the theory first and then show it in practice but vice versa: it first presents the practice and then deduces the theory. Sin found its way into this world through the tempting question "Did God really say"? (Gen 3:1), thereby doubting God's goodness. Sin is thus an expression of the will, opposing the will of God. Both the Ten Commandments (Ex 20:1-17) and the Sermon on the Mount (Matt 5-7) are excellent mirrors of one's sinfulness. If someone lives without the Word of God, he obviously does not know God's will and so lives automatically and permanently in sin, often without being aware of it. The first word for sin (Hebr. *chattath*) mentioned in the Bible (Gen 4:7) means *missing the target*; the Greek *hamartia* is translated similarly. Further meanings of the word sin are turning away, distortion (Hebr. *awon*), wickedness, evilness (Hebr. *raa*) violence (Hebr. *chamas*) evil way of thinking (Hebr. *rascha*). Even the absence of righteousness is sin: "Woe to him who builds his palace by unrighteousness" (Jer 22:13). In the NT the corresponding verse is: "Everything that does not come from faith is sin" (Rom 14:23). *Hermann Bezzel* called the isolation of man from God sin. In John 16:9 Jesus identifies the fundamental sin of man as indifference toward Him: "Men do not believe in me." Sin is the great disrupter in the relationship between God and man. Whoever does not experience correction through conversion and forgiveness (1 John 1:9) experiences the consequences of having missed the goal according to the infallible law "For the wages of sin is [eternal] death" (Rom 6:23). For many people health occupies first place on the list of priorities, but they disregard the worst illness of all: sin – the illness which ends in death.

QL 6: *Does the Bible allow unmarried couples to live together? When is a couple to be considered married? From the couple's decision to stay together? After first intercourse? After the registry or the church wedding?*

AL 6: To answer these questions, which are becoming increasingly important in our times, five biblical guidelines should be mentioned. In the method of biblical interpretation we will use the solution cannot be derived from a single verse but is crystallized from the context of several basic statements (see Interpretation Principles IP5 and IP6 in the Appendix, Part II).

1. *Marriage and sexuality:* God instituted marriage in His creation order. It is His will and His good idea: "It is not good for the man to be alone. I will make a helper suitable for him" (Gen 2:18). Marriage is intended as a lifelong partnership (Matt 19:6) which, according to the wedding vows, shall last "as long as both shall live." When God arranged this partnership of man and woman, the Creator said: "For this reason a man will leave his father and mother and be united to his wife, and they will become one flesh" (Gen 2:24). This "becoming-one-flesh" firstly refers to the physical, sexual union. This short formula, however, encompasses the entire person and hence soul and spirit, too. Two people with previously separate lives come together in the most intimate partnership of all. They grow together in their emotions and thoughts as well as on a spiritual and physical level. Sexuality is a gift from God and the marital relationship is not intended solely for the purpose of propagation according to Scripture:

> "Do not deprive each other except by mutual consent and for a time, so that you may devote yourselves to prayer" (1 Cor 7:5).

> "May your fountain be blessed, and may you rejoice in the wife of your youth. A loving doe, a graceful deer – may her breasts satisfy you always, may you ever be captivated by her love" (Prov 5:18-19).

> "Enjoy life with your wife, whom you love" (Eccl 9:9).

The Bible shows us how to deal correctly with sexuality. It is distinct from prudishness (Song of Songs 4) as well as lust (Jer 5:8). Love and respect are the crucial prerequisites (Col 3:19; 1 Pet 3:7).

2. *Marriage and the church are founded by God:* In this world there are many different forms of human community, of which marriage and family, church and state (Rom 13:1-7) are in accordance with God's will. The church of Jesus Christ and marriage, however, are two special institutions defined by God and are not, despite popular opinion, human inventions. Both communities are therefore attacked by a godless world (1 Tim 4:3; Rev 2:9). Right from the beginning, there has been no human culture without marriage. The institution of marriage has never been outdated and will endure in spite of anti-marriage trends and in spite of human failure. Marriage is part of God's loving and caring plan for man. Similarly the church, in accordance with Jesus' promise, will never be overpowered by the gates of hell (Matt 16:18).

3. *Marriage as a parable:* The Bible often describes faith and the relationship between God and man by way of the most intimate trusting human relationship imaginable, marriage. "As a young man marries a maiden ... as a bridegroom rejoices over his bride, so will your God rejoice over you" (Is 62:5). This is why marriage is chosen as a parable (Greek *mystaerion* = mystery) for the relationship between Christ and His church: "... just as Christ loved the church and gave himself up for her ... in this same way husbands ought to love their wives." (Eph 5:25,28). God's Word says about this analogy: "This is a profound mystery" (Eph 5:32). Already the fact that marriage is used to characterize the eternal communion with Christ, indicates that marriage is a partnership for life. Each divorced marriage produces a distortion of God's ideas and destroys the trait of the parable. This also explains the uncompromising attitude of Jesus with regard to divorce (Matt 19:6-9).

4. *Prostitution as parable:* If a marriage, lived in love and faithfulness, is a symbol for the relationship between God and His people, then the Bible describes the falling away from God and the worship of foreign gods and idols as adultery or prostitution:

> "Have you seen what faithless Israel has done? She has gone up on every high hill and under every spreading tree and has committed adultery there … she defiled the land and committed adultery with stone and wood" (Jer 3:6,9).

> "Your adulteries and lustful neighings, your shameless prostitution! I have seen your detestable acts on the hills and in the fields" (Jer 13:27).

5. *What is fornication (KJV; NIV = "sexual immorality")?* The English words *fornication, prostitution* or *whoremongering* have only one expression in the language of the New Testament, the Greek *porneia,* from which our word *pornography* is derived. *Fornicators* (KJV; Greek = *pornos*) are listed alongside adulterers and homosexuals in the NT (e.g. 1 Cor 6:9). *Porneia* is given as a generic term for *any kind* of satisfaction of sexual drive outside of marriage as instituted by God (e.g. 1 Cor 6:18; 1 Thess 4:3). This includes:

- premarital sexual intercourse (Deut 22:18)
- sexual intercourse with a woman other than one's wife (Lev 18:20; Jer 5:8-9; Matt 5:32)
- homosexuality (Gen 19:5; Rom 1:26-27; 1 Tim 1:10)
- incest (1 Cor 5:1)
- sexual relations with animals (Lev 18:23).

Those that practise *porneia* are subject to serious judgment by God:

> "Neither the sexually immoral nor idolaters nor adulterers nor male prostitutes nor homosexual offenders … will inherit the kingdom of God" (1 Cor 6:9-10).

"God will judge the adulterer and all the sexually immoral" (Hebr 13:4).

"Outside are ... the sexually immoral, the murderers, the idolaters and everyone who loves and practises falsehood" (Rev 22:15).

Conclusion: According to these biblical principles the answer is obvious: the co-habitation of unmarried couples is thus – just like pre- or extramarital sexual intercourse – called sexual immorality (fornication) and excludes us from the kingdom of God, unless those involved turn away from their sinful life and repent (see Appendix, Part I, Point 10).

When does a marriage begin? With the increasing alienation of mankind from God's Commandments it is noticeable that more and more unmarried couples co-habit and live in a marriage-like but non-committal relationship. Even if one does not see any difference between their partnership and a marriage, the truth is that they are not married. We have already mentioned how God regards these relationships in point 5.

From the testimony of the Bible, we see that marriage does not begin

- *with the intention of marriage*: Jacob wanted to take Rachel as his wife. When the contracted seven years prior to the marriage were past, Jacob said to his father-in-law Laban: "Give me my wife. My time is completed, and I want to lie with her" (Gen 29:21). This means sexual intercourse. Two things emerge from this passage: Prior to marriage, Jacob did not have sexual relations with Rachel, and the marriage came into effect from the public feast onward.

- *if a couple had sexual relations*: If a man slept with a girl in Israel, he had to marry her and – as was custom then – pay the bride price (Deut 22:28-29). Intimate relations prior to an officially contracted marriage were not allowed.

Definition of when a marriage begins: A marriage is considered binding – before God as well – once man and wife have gone through the official wedding ritual customary in their society.

This definition can be reconstructed for all biblical examples of marriages. Here we come across the following scriptural interpretation principle: from a wealth of single events the common denominator is extracted as biblical teaching. In the same way this definition can be applied to every far-off tribe with its own rituals recognized within that society as well as in our culture where the registry office ceremony is customary. In all cases it is important that the people in their environment know clearly and officially that here two people have been joined in matrimony. They are thus no longer available to others. If a man looks at a married woman (or a married man at another woman or vice versa) and covets her (him) then, according to the Sermon on the Mount, he (she) is an adulterer (Matt 5:28). Jesus told the woman at Jacob's well that the man she had was not her husband (John 4:18). If she had been married to him by way of an official contraction of marriage, Jesus would not have spoken to her the way he did. Nowhere does the Bible lay down the external form a wedding should take, but there is a definite wedding day and from then on man and wife belong together officially. The external form during Abraham's time (Gen 24:66) was different to that of Samson's time (7 day wedding celebration; Judges 14:10-20) or that of Jesus' time (wedding at Cana; John 2:1-11). In South Africa, for example, only the magistrate or licensed marriage officer is empowered to conduct a marriage which is then valid before God.

QL 7: *Believing does not mean* knowing *– how then can you presume faith to be a certainty?*

AL 7: Numerous scholars have pondered the question of faith, offering very different points of view. However, their ideas do not represent the result of neutral thought processes but personal opinions.

Critical points of view: The atheist *Theo Löbsack* maintains: "Faith defends preconceived opinions and rejects scientific findings if they do not correspond to these opinions. Thus, in the final analysis, faith is the arch-enemy of science." *Kant* said in a similarly critical vein: "I would have to negate knowledge to make room for faith." This unbiblical viewpoint made him the pioneer of various philosophical schools which diametrically oppose faith. The motto on a wall of the new High School in Norf, Germany, "Trust no one whose god is in heaven" is the final consequence of this critical type of reasoning.

Positive points of view: Probably the greatest physicist of all times, *Sir Isaac Newton*, said: "He who thinks half-heartedly will not believe in God; but he who really thinks has to believe in God." With the same certainty, the famous mathematician *Blaise Pascal* testified: "Just as all things speak about God to those that know Him, and reveal Him to those that love Him, they also hide Him from all those that neither seek nor know Him".

These two contrasting viewpoints clearly document that faith is not a function of ignorance but depends entirely on the individual's preconceived attitude and ideas. This is not changed by philosophical reflections, but only by turning to Jesus Christ, an act which the Bible calls conversion. To the unbeliever, questions of faith are foolishness (1 Cor 1:18) and he cannot understand them (1 Cor 2:14). The person enthused with Christ, however, will be guided into all truth

(John 16:13); his faith has a solid foundation (1 Cor 3:11) and is very certain:

"Now faith is being sure of what we hope for and certain of what we do not see" (Hebr 11:1).

QL 8: *Is an external sign necessary for rebirth?*

AL 8: *Conversion* and *rebirth* are two words which describe the process of salvation. Conversion is thus the human and rebirth the divine side of one and the same process. During a nocturnal talk Jesus said to Nicodemus: "No one can see the kingdom of God unless he is born again" (John 3:3). Rebirth is thus necessary to secure admission to God's presence. To be reborn is a passive process just like natural birth. By natural birth we enter this earthly life and become citizens of this world. Similarly, our heavenly citizenship is obtained through birth. Since we have all been born once, the Bible talks about this second, spiritual, birth which gives us the right of access to the heavenly (eternal) life, as *rebirth*.

When we repent, we turn away from our old sinful life and when we are converted we turn to Christ. Everyone who turns to God with their whole being, will one day be with God. God answers the desires of our heart by granting us new eternal life; this is our rebirth. This process has nothing to do with an external sign, but the new attitude to life will be obvious in the visible fruit of the Spirit: "Love, joy, peace, patience, kindness, goodness, faithfulness, gentleness and self-control" (Gal 5:22).

QL 9: *You address us here as if God Himself had sent you. What gives you the right to do so?* (Asked at a lecture in a prison)

AL 9: I am pleased that you have asked this question in such a challenging way as it is important to be accountable for what I say. If you are waiting to hear the gospel proclaimed by an angel from heaven, then you are waiting in vain. God Himself accomplished salvation through Jesus Christ; but He has entrusted the proclamation of this fact to men. It complies with the will of God that the disciples of Jesus take up this task of making disciples and teaching them the ways of the Lord (Matt 28:19-20). We can act in the name of the Lord who has made heaven and earth, "for we are God's fellow-workers" (1 Cor 3:9). This task has been entrusted to all who believe in Jesus Christ. One day we will have to account for what we have done with the gospel entrusted to us (Luke 19:11-27). The representative of a government with the highest credentials abroad is the Ambassador. He is authorized, accredited and sent to represent his government in full. The Son of God has put us in the exalted position of ambassadors in order to spread the gospel, for the NT clearly states: "We are therefore Christ's ambassadors, as though God were making his appeal through us – we implore you on Christ's behalf: Be reconciled to God!" (2 Cor 5:20). Jesus said in Luke 10:16: "He who listens to you listens to me." Therefore we are legitimized not through ourselves but through God.

QL 10: *What do you think of genetic engineering?*

AL 10: Genetic engineering makes it possible to recombine genes in new ways. It allows us to manipulate the DNA of living beings quickly and effectively, and to use it for particular aims. The focus of current research in the field of gene technology is on the construction of bacterial cells, which, through the introduction of foreign genes (from a mammal or a human, for example) become factories for products which are of medical or technical interest (hormones or vaccines, for example). The first such genetically engineered product was the hormone *insulin*, which is essential in the treatment of diabetes. The process involves introducing the particular gene that produces a normal amount of insulin in healthy human beings to *E. Coli* bacteria. The insulin produced in this way is therefore identical with that produced in the human body. Long-term goals of genetic engineering include improving the nutritional value of cultivated plants and making them more resistant to infection and herbicides, as well as curing inherited diseases through the introduction of an additional intact gene into the DNA strand of a human. The value of this new technology is unequivocal. However, we need to remember that any technology is ambivalent; a hammer can be used to put a nail into a wall, but also to break someone's skull. The long-term results of even well-intentioned technical applications are unpredictable. This is particularly true of genetic engineering.

It is well known that the building of the tower at Babel was linked to the judgment of confusion of languages. Far less well-known is the fact that God has given man up to his own actions: "nothing they plan to do will be impossible for them" (Gen 11:6). God permits mankind to do things they ought not to attempt. It would have been better for mankind if they had been unable to build gas chambers in order to kill people on a massive scale, or to develop atom bombs in order to wipe out cities, or to dream up ideas which enslave men. It has become possible for man to fly to the moon and to transplant organs. But man can also manipulate genes.

The man with no relationship to God considers himself autonomous and his actions know no limits. His own deeds will sit in judgment on him. The man who believes in God will look for biblical standards and refrain from doing certain things even though they would be possible. In the command "multiply" (Gen 1:28) God gives man a share in the creation process. In the sexual allocation of man and woman, God gave the prerequisites for this creation process but God still remains the Creator: "For you created my inmost being; you knit me together in my mother's womb" (Ps 139:13). By way of gene manipulation we change the process God gave: genes transferred to the fertilized egg can be passed on to subsequent generations. This intervention cannot be reversed and contains incalculable dangers. *Ch. Flämig's* utopian vision sees the goal of genetics as the creation of a superman: "The best minds of mankind will ... develop genetic methods, which invent new properties, organs and biosystems which serve the interests, the happiness and glory of those god-like creatures, whose puny forerunners we miserable creatures of today are." ('Die genetische Manipulation des Menschen', [Genetic manipulation of man] taken from 'Politik und Zeitgeschichte' B3/1985, pp. 3-17). With such an objective, man becomes a Prometheus who despises God:

> "Here I sit, forming men
> in my image.
> A species similar to me,
> that suffers, that cries,
> that enjoys and is happy
> and that ignores you
> like I do." *(Johann Wolfgang von Goethe)*

QL 11: *What did Jesus do with mosquitoes and horseflies? Did He swat them?*

AL 11: *Albert Schweitzer* (1875 – 1965) coined the well-known phrase "awe of life" which – if applied consistently to the human race – would prevent the annual number of 80 million abortions world-wide. *Schweitzer* went even further, though, and tried never to squash an insect in the jungle. In Hinduism, too, no animal may be killed on principle (*ahimsa*). They believe that after death a person could be reincarnated in the form of an animal. As a result, India has 8 times as many rats as people. The amount of food consumed by these rats has become an insurmountable problem; the damage done is indescribable. The biblical commandment "You shall not murder" (Ex 20:13) refers only to mankind. The commandment does not apply to animals since they were given explicitly to man as food (Gen 9:3). Even the intensification by Jesus of the injunction against murder in the Sermon on the Mount (Matt 5:21-26) is in no way extended to include the animal world as well.

The above question draws Jesus into a hinduistic behavioural pattern or the behavioural pattern of *Albert Schweitzer* and *Francis of Assisi,* who punished himself if he happened to squash an insect. In the Bible, God shows us how to deal correctly with the animal kingdom. In the initial creation everything was deemed "[to be] very good" (Gen 1:31). There were thus no illnesses, no death, no harmful insects and no dangerous animals. After the Fall, the animal kingdom, too, was deeply affected, the effects being evident in each species in a different way. There is the category of clean and unclean animals (Gen 7:2). There is furthermore a distinction between savage (Lev 26:6) and useful animals; the protection of the latter is even mentioned in the Ten Commandments (Ex 20:10,17). In Deuteronomy 25:4, God gives the oxen who is treading out the corn the right to receive food. Other animals who initially had a positive role with regard to man became real pests. The Bible mentions in particular locusts, beetles, caterpillars, frogs and insects. If they appear en masse, they are God's judgment. (Ex 10:12; Ps 78:45-46; Ps 105:30-34; Joel 2:25; Amos 4:9). In the same way, snakes and scorpions represent a danger to man against which God can protect (Num 21:8-9; Luke 10:19) or which God can use to overpower man in order to judge (Num 21:6; 1 Kings 12:11).
Most illnesses are caused by micro-organisms (viruses, bacteria, parasites). If Jesus were to heal all illnesses (Matt 4:23)

then He would also have to eradicate these creatures which threaten and harm man. We paint a distorted picture of Jesus Christ if we attribute to Him an unrealistic assessment of the fallen world. He commands with authority potentially destructive powers such as wind and waves (Matt 8:27), illness and death (Matt 8:3; John 11:43-44), demons and evil spirits (Luke 11:14). Jesus came to us as the Son of God and as man at the same time. He was "made in human likeness. And being found in appearance as a man" (Phil 2:7-8), i.e. He was exposed to the same situations as other people and therefore also pests such as mosquitoes, gnats, horseflies, flies and the like. The Bible does not explicitly recount how He dealt with them. But from what we have said above, we may nevertheless assume that he would have shooed them away as well as killed them.

7. What You always Wanted to Know about Heaven but never Dared to Ask

A student approached me after a presentation in the city of Mainz, Germany. I noticed her determination to get an answer as she said, *"You've just been talking about time and life after death. But what is eternity exactly?"* I was surprised to be asked this question by such an attractive young woman. She was so full of life, why didn't she just postpone the question as many other people do? I said to her, *"I'm interested to know why this question is so important to you."* She replied, *"I was recently diagnosed as having a hereditary heart condition. As it stands, the doctors have given me just a few more years to live. So you see, I **have** to know what eternity is."*

I immediately realized that this was neither a theoretical, nor a quibbling theological question, but a very existential one. I was moved by the clarity and decisiveness with which this young woman was looking for an answer to this fundamental question. Before I could answer her she made it clear what she didn't want to hear.

She said, *"I can imagine what hell is like. I have read* Sartre, *and he described it in one piece quite evocatively: people are locked in a room and cannot understand each other. They can never leave the room. Never. That is hell. I can imagine that. But what is heaven like? That is what I would like to know."* She continued, *"And please don't tell me it 'll be singing Hallelujah or praising God unendingly. I can't imagine having to sing forever. Nor do I desire to praise God continually for the rest of eternity. But I know eternity is our goal in life. It **has** to be something I can look forward to."*

I tried, in my answer, to describe heaven as a place full of joy and love. She interrupted me right away, *"That is not precise enough for me. How could I rejoice in a place where there is nothing but joy? One can only feel joy as such when one has experienced its opposite, sadness or anger."*

The young woman challenged me to examine the question more intensively and to answer exactly, according to the Bible. I will never forget that conversation, as it led me to shift the focus of my presentations to the theme of heaven. What a blessing it would be if more people asked such specific questions about life after death!

At the end of our conversation, she said, *"Why is so little preached or written about eternity? Why do most sermons only deal with this life? People are being denied something crucial."* She was right, and because of that encounter in Mainz, I have included a chapter in this book which deals with the question of life after death in detail.

The young woman spoke of both heaven and hell. We, too, will deal with both places, as Jesus preached vigorously and repeatedly on both subjects.

What about hell?

During the Vietnam war, a minister went to comfort a dying soldier. The soldier knew he had only minutes left to live, only minutes before he would be faced with eternity. There was only one question burning in his soul: "Minister, is there a hell?" The minister's answer was a clear, "No." The soldier's reply was equally clear: "If there is no hell, then we don't need you here at all. You should just go home! But, if there really **is** a hell, then you've misled everyone you have spoken to. You're just lying to us here."

Jesus clearly speaks of hell as a place that exists. His intention is never to scare us, but to warn us and to invite us into the other, equally real place – heaven.

In the Sermon on the Mount, Jesus warns us: "If your right eye causes you to sin, gouge it out and throw it away. It is better for you to lose one part of your body than for your whole body to be thrown into hell. And if your right hand causes you to sin, cut it off and throw it away. It is better for you to lose one part of your body than for your whole body to go into hell" (Matt 5,29-30).

Let us take yet another passage from the Gospel of Matthew: "Do not be afraid of those who kill the body but cannot kill the soul. Rather, be afraid of the one who can destroy both soul and body in hell" (Matt 10:28). Who sends people to hell? It is certainly not the devil, although that might seem likely at first. The devil himself is condemned and will be judged (Rev 12:10; Rev 20:10). The Judge will make the Last Judgment, and God has set the Lord Jesus to be that Judge. As we read in Matthew 25:41: "Then he [= Jesus] will say to those on his left, 'Depart from me, you who are cursed, into the eternal fire prepared for the devil and his angels'."

Towards whom are the warnings about hell directed? Who is being addressed? I always thought that they were directed at the faithless, the outsiders, the thieves and criminals. However, in almost all cases Jesus directs His warnings about hell towards the faithful. He only addresses the Pharisees on occasion, but when he does, Jesus is especially strict with them because of their self-righteousness. They do not receive a *warning,* because hell is *a certain end* for them: "Woe to you, teachers of the law and Pharisees, you hypocrites! You shut the kingdom of heaven in men's faces. You yourselves do not enter, nor will you let those enter who are trying to (Matt 23:13)."

The British author *David Pawson* once compiled a list of those deeds which, according to the Bible, lead to hell. This list contains 120 points and names, among others, the following groups of people:

- the adulterers
- the homosexuals
- the debauched
- the liars
- the miserly
- the proud
- those who follow astrology
- the cowardly
- the slothful
- ...

In the Parable of the Talents, the man who receives one talent says: "Master, ... I knew that you are a hard man, harvesting where you have not sown and gathering where you have not scattered seed. So I was afraid and went out and hid your talent in the ground. See, here is what belongs to you" (Matt 25:24-25). His Lord answers him, "You wicked, lazy servant! So you knew that I harvest where I have not sown and gather where I have not scattered seed?" (Matt 25:26). The text ends with the punishment of rejection: "And throw that worthless servant outside, into the darkness, where there will be weeping and gnashing of teeth" (Matt 25:30). The Bible defines this place of darkness as hell. This servant is neither an atheist, nor a bad person in the usual sense. He is one who knows Jesus. That is why he addresses Jesus as "Master." Despite this, he is lost. And why? Because he is lazy!

In the Sermon on the Mount, Jesus gives a serious warning to those who habitually have His name on their lips, but will never see the glory of God: "Not everyone who says to me 'Lord, Lord' will enter the kingdom of heaven, but only he who does the will of my Father who is in heaven" (Matt 7:21). The Parable of the Ten Virgins is also about the faithful. But five of them were to find that "the door was shut" (Matt 25:10). Why? Their way of life reflected more the customs of the time than the Commandments of God, and Jesus Christ was no longer the centre of their lives. That is why they hear the unexpected words of Jesus: "I tell you the truth, I don't know you" (Matt 25:12).

On the third of June 1998, possibly the most tragic railway accident in the history of Germany occurred when a broken wheel caused a high-speed train ICE to derail and slam into a concrete bridge in the small town of Eschede near Hannover. One hundred people died in that accident. On the twenty-first of June, a funeral service for the victims was held in Celle, with the President and the Chancellor of Germany both in attendance, as well as the friends and families of the victims. Of course, in a situation like this, a sermon should offer comfort and support to the relatives. However, the sermon should still be truthful. Both Catholic and Protestant clergy preached that the victims of the accident would all go to heaven. That is not right. We do not know how many of the deceased really knew the Lord Jesus. It would surely be a percentage similar to that among people in our neighbourhood and at our place of work. Unfortunately, there are only few who have truly taken the Lord Jesus into their lives. According to the Bible, only they will be received into heaven (John 3:3).

In a similar situation involving an accident at the time of Jesus, he comments on those on whom the tower of Siloam fell (Luke 13:4). Jesus' answer is worth noting: "But unless you repent, you too will all perish" (Luke 13:5). He uses the event not to bless the dead, but to preach to the living.

One preacher writes: "People used to be afraid of hell. Today, they are afraid of talking about it." One can only speak of being saved where there is danger to be saved from. Because there is a hell, we need a saviour. This saviour is the Lord Jesus: "For God did not send his son into the world to condemn the world, **but to save the world through him** [= Jesus]" (John 3:17). Jesus Himself is the gate to heaven: "I am the gate; whoever enters through me will be saved" (John 10:9).

What do we know about heaven?

The following quip about heaven is from the German poet *Heinrich Heine* (1797 – 1856): "We shall let the angels and sparrows have heaven" (from *Wintermärchen*). Hopefully, he changed his mind after he had written that line, or he is regretting his eternal isolation in the place of darkness.

Heaven as a concept is used in many sayings and forms of speech to describe various aspects of life. When one is happy, one is "in seventh heaven." Something that is very good is "heavenly." There is even a delicious flavour of ice cream called "Heavenly Hash." For most people the only knowledge they have about heaven is what they hear in everyday expressions like that. Is that all that there is to say about heaven?

So what do we know about heaven?

On closer examination it becomes clear that the idioms fall far short of a satisfactory description of heaven. God has revealed a number of specific details about heaven to us. The Bible is the only authoritative source of information – anything else is pure speculation and the product of human imagination. The Bible often addresses this topic which is the greatest goal given to mankind. Numerous aspects of heaven become clear when we read the Word of God and apply reason to the understanding of it. In our study we will occasionally refer to relevant aspects of our life here on earth for comparison.

While we can test whether the Bible is right about earthly things, we have to accept what it says about heaven in faith. That is why Jesus said, "I have spoken to you of earthly things and you do not believe; how then will you believe if I speak of heavenly things?" (John 3:12).

It is impossible to grasp that this eternal and almighty God would like to share our company in heaven. He sends His servants to invite all peoples and nations until all are in attendance: "Then the master told his servant, 'Go out to the roads and country lanes and make them come in, so that my house will be full'" (Luke 14:23).

We have been given an unmistakable description of the way to heaven so that we don't miss this greatest of opportunities. Jesus states in John 14:6: "No one comes to the Father except through me." This word is fulfilled in heaven. Only those people who have been saved by the Lord Jesus will reach heaven (John 3:36; 1 John 5:13).

In the ten points which follow we will look at the nature of heaven in more detail.

H1: Heaven is the place where we will be perfectly happy

The French philosopher *Jean Jacques Rousseau* (1712 – 1778) does not get at the heart of the meaning of happiness when he remarks that "happiness is having a healthy bank account, a good cook and excellent digestion." *Voltaire* (1694 – 1778) states that "total happiness cannot be known, it is not created for man." This philosopher is also wrong. Jesus can make us really happy. When Jesus talks about being happy, or blessed, it means much more than what we understand by the word 'happy' today. The eternal component is important. Jesus saw his main task as saving humans (Matt 18:11). Those who are saved are happy because they are given the glory of heaven. This supreme happiness begins here on earth and will be perfected in heaven: "Therefore he is able to save completely those who come to God through him" (Hebr 7:25). Only those who are saved know real joy and happiness.

In heaven, the place without sin, happiness will be perfect and everlasting, for none of the negative aspects of this world will tarnish life there.

Many people must bear unspeakable suffering on this earth. The bookshelves of the world are full of accounts of suffering and innumerable questions as to why an almighty and loving God can allow them to happen.

Ever since the Flood, humanity has not remained immune to catastrophes, large and small. On the first of November 1755, an earthquake in Portugal turned Lisbon into a pile of rubble. Sixty thousand people died. This event did not fit into the view of the world held by most people at the time. Greatly moved and critical, the German author *Goethe* wrote, "God the Creator and Keeper of Heaven and Earth did not show himself to be fatherly in his punishment of both the righteous and unrighteous."

There is no shortage of accounts of terrible suffering. The high number of victims does not matter, whether six million or sixty thousand. The death of even one person is enough for us to ask: "How could God allow this to happen?" In the life after death, all traces of suffering will be erased. There, nothing will remind us of pain, war, hate or death. "He will wipe every tear from their eyes. There will be no more death or mourning or crying or pain, for the old order of things has passed away" (Rev 21:4).

Our body will then be freed from all disease and frailty. It will never have to fight with germs, viruses, infections, diseases of the heart or lungs. There will be no such things as hospitals or prisons. There will be no more need for doctors, nurses, police officers, prison wardens or gravediggers.

Once we are in heaven, nobody will want to return to earth. The time of burdens and worries will be over forever.

The Prussian king *Frederick the Great* (1712–1786) named his castle in the city of Potsdam near Berlin *Sanssoussi* (without worries) but led a life full of worries. *Sanssoussi* would only be a correct description of heaven. Heaven is the only place where there is no fighting, no war, no hate, no unfaithfulness, no worries and no broken hearts.

H2: Heaven is a place of pleasure for the senses

We humans pay a lot of money just to be able to see or hear something special.

- Outrageous prices are paid to be at the opening ceremonies of the Olympics, for example. At the 1996 Summer Games in Atlanta, tickets cost over one thousand dollars each, not to mention the even more inflated prices of the ticket scalpers.
- The concerts of famous conductors are popular among those who wish to treat their ears to something special. The first night performances of plays are just as sought-after.
- For tennis or football fans, the finals in Wimbledon or the Superbowl game are a special treat.

All that we now consider attractive, beautiful to look at or a pleasure to hear pales in comparison to heaven. The Bible describes both the wisdom of God as well as heaven fittingly when it says: "No eye has seen, no ear has heard, no mind has conceived what God has prepared for those who love him" (1 Cor 2:9).

Not just our eyes and ears but all our senses will be satisfied in heaven. That includes for example, our tastebuds but also much, much more – everything that makes us feel good will be available in heaven: love, peace, joy, friendliness, goodness.

H3: Heaven is the place of everlasting celebration

How do we prepare for a celebration? The yearly presentation of Oscars took place in Los Angeles on March 23 1998. It was a gala party of film, to which previous Oscar-winners, sponsors and many actors were invited. One magazine described the Oscar time-stress as follows:

> "Pre-Oscar:
> three months to go: book appointment with hairdresser
> one month to go: visit spa
> 10 days to go: get hair cut
> 3 days to go: visit tanning salon
>
> On Oscar Day:
> morning: work out, shower, wash hair, eat light meal
> lunch: wait for hair stylist
> afternoon: wait for make-up artist
> 4pm exactly: guests must be in auditorium
>
> Then the doors close. The dice have been cast. 'And the Oscar goes to…'"

As this example shows, the preparation for a celebration which only lasts a few hours can take tremendous effort. Most of the effort is spent on beauty. In this world, everything deteriorates, and beauty fades. The effort to compensate with artificial means increases with age. None of this will be necessary in heaven. There we will all be beautiful. More precisely: we will all be *glorious*, and glorious is the superlative of beautiful.

Jesus is described even in the Old Testament when we read, "The Lord reigns, he is robed in majesty" (Ps 93:1). He is the "glorious Lord Jesus" (James 2:1). On His return, He will come in all His power and glory (Matt 24:30). In John 17:22, He prays to His Father: "I have given them the glory that you gave me."

God has a problem: How can He make us humans understand the glory and festivity of heaven? Jesus explains in a parable: "The kingdom of heaven is like a king who prepared a wedding banquet for his son" (Matt 22:2). A wedding is the most beautiful celebration on earth. Everything is prepared, down to the last detail:

- beloved guests are invited
- the best food and finest drink will be served
- no problems will be discussed on the special day
- the bride will look more beautiful than ever before, and will wear the most beautiful and most precious dress of her life
- everyone will have a good time

In using this well-known picture, Jesus tries to describe heaven to us as an unusually beautiful celebration. At the Last Supper, He says to His disciples: "I tell you, I will not drink of this fruit of the vine from now on until that day when I drink it anew with you in my Father's kingdom" (Matt 26:29).

That wine will be like nothing we have ever tasted here on earth. I also believe we will eat in heaven. How else are we to interpret Luke 12:37: "He [= Jesus] will dress himself to serve, will have them recline at the table and will come and wait on them."

We can safely assume that it will be a richly set table. The earthly concepts of "costly" and "precious" are too weak to describe what we will find in heaven. But it is clear that heaven is festive.

Now comes the surprise: Heaven is not just comparable to a wedding, but is the place where a real wedding occurs. In Revelation 19:7 we read, "Let us rejoice and be glad and give him glory! For the wedding of the Lamb has come, and his bride has made herself ready." Jesus Himself is the groom, and all who have been saved through Him are the bride.

Those who are invited can consider themselves happy. In the Parable of the Lost Son, we read that "they began to celebrate" (Luke 15:24). Joy is everlasting in heaven; we cannot estimate the degree of this happiness.

H4: Heaven is a beautiful place

Jesus said in the Sermon on the Mount, concerning this Creation, "See how the lilies of the field grow. They do not labor or spin. Yet I tell you that not even Solomon in all his splendor was dressed like one of these" (Matt 6:28-29). The creation displays the Creator's love of beauty which mankind cannot imitate. God is the originator of all that is beautiful.

After much suffering, God blessed Job: "And he also had seven sons and three daughters. The first daughter he named Jemimah [= little dove], the second Keziah [= cinnamon

blossom] and the third Keren-Happuch [= precious vessel]"
(Job 42:13-15). The beauty of Job's daughters is especially
emphasized. They would have won any Miss World Com-
petition.

Of Jesus Himself, the Creator in person, it is said in Psalm
45:2: "You are the most excellent of men and your lips have
been anointed with grace, since God has blessed you for ever."
When He is sacrificed on the cross for the sin of humanity,
however, He gives up His beauty, as we can read in Isaiah 53:2,
"He had no beauty or majesty to attract us to him, nothing in
his appearance that we should desire him".

Jesus has always been described as beautiful and perfect. In
Isaiah 33:17 it is written: "Your eyes will see the king in his
beauty." The well-known German song *Fairest Lord Jesus*
expresses this aspect especially well:

> Fairest Lord Jesus, Ruler of all nature
> O Thou of God and man the Son
> Thee will I cherish
> Thee will I honour
> Thou my soul's glory, joy and crown.
>
> Fair are the meadows, fairer still the woodlands
> Robed in the blooming garb of spring
> Jesus is fairer
> Jesus is purer
> Who makes the troubled heart to sing.
>
> Fair is the sunshine, fairer still the moonlight
> And fair the twinkling, starry host
> Jesus shines brighter
> Jesus shines purer
> Than all the angels Heav'n can boast.

...

Beautiful Saviour! Lord of the nations!
Son of God and son of man!
Glory and honour,
Praise, adoration
Now and forevermore be thine.

(From the German
"Schönster Herr Jesus", 1677)

If God's love for beauty is evident even in this Creation, in the form of every snowflake, each lily, orchid and the countless blooms of other flowers or the luxurious plumage of some birds, how much more fitting it is to have beauty as one of the most important attributes of heaven!

Many people seek beauty on this earth. Surgeons who perform facelifts are in great demand. An entire industry specializing in the making and selling of beauty-enhancing or beauty-preserving products is assured of thriving business. Yet, even the most renowned of this world's Beauty Queens will see their beauty fade. Everything on earth is perishable (Rom 8:20).

The Empress *Elisabeth of Austria*, better known by her nickname *Sissi* (1837–1898) was known in the 19th century as the most beautiful woman in Europe. She was so vain that she would not have her portrait painted after her thirtieth birthday, let alone have photographs taken of her. The German author *Annelie Fried* writes, "Female television hosts reach their date of expiry at the age of forty. After that, the nation watching from their living rooms counts the wrinkles."

Heaven, in contrast, is a place of everlasting beauty. All who have gone there will stay beautiful forever. When we become like Jesus (1 John 3:2), we will also receive His beauty. The earthly value of looking "forever young" is not nearly adequate to describe the heavenly ideal.

H5: Heaven is where our lives will be fulfilled

Most of mankind live below the poverty line. Forty thousand children die daily because they do not have enough to eat. Others are rich; they can afford whatever worldly goods their heart desires and yet are unhappy. Many suffer from depression and worries, or are simply bored.

Jesus is aware of both emotional and physical human needs. "When he saw the crowds, he had compassion on them, because they were harassed and helpless, like sheep without a shepherd" (Matt 9:36). He wants to help especially here; that is why in John 10:10 He gives as the main reason of His Coming: "I have come that they may have life, and have it to the full."

Converting to Jesus changes our lives so fundamentally here on earth that we can clearly see the difference between the old and the new life (Rom 6:4; Col 2:6; 1 Pet 4:3). However, it is once we are in heaven, that our lives become completely fulfilled. There, we will know for the first time, what true quality of life means.

A critic once said that he would never feel like sitting on a cloud and playing a harp for ten thousand years. That is a fabricated picture of life after death, one which we do not find in the Bible.

Heaven is life in abundance. The concept of scarcity is not known in heaven. There is nothing there in need of improvement. Boredom is also unknown, for heaven is complete and offers a life of fulfillment.

While hell can be described as a place of lasting unfulfilled desires, there will be no more yearning in heaven. This does not necessarily mean that all our earthly desires will find their fulfillment in heaven, but that the richness of heaven will be shared with us – a richness which we cannot even imagine – a richness which will make earthly desires superfluous.

When we experience beautiful moments here on earth, we want to hold on to them. That is what *Goethe* describes when he writes, *"Stay but, thou art so fair!"* Cameras and videos capture the past; they do not represent life. Heaven, on the other hand, could be described as *everlasting simultaneousness*. Nothing is constrained by mortality. Everything is permanent.

Here on earth, we can only be in one place at one time. Each move brings separation from people we love. Saying "good-bye" is often painful. In heaven, we will never have to say "good-bye."

H6: Heaven is a home for us

The architects of this world continually invent new types of buildings. *Jörn Utzon*, the architect of the Opera House in Sydney, Australia, used a peeled orange as his inspiration. We admire powerful palaces of glass and high-reaching towers of concrete. An architect once wrote that "architecture unites the demands of art with technical perfection. Architecture has been the expression of humanity's yearning for the eternal. Besides architectural works of genius, monuments such as the Great Wall of China and the Pyramids of Gizeh count as some of the longest-lasting works of human hands."

In a nineteenth-century spa resort on the North Sea island of Juist, a special building was reopened in 1998 after massive reconstruction. The *White Castle by the Sea*, as it is called, located on a high dune, is the first sight on approaching the island by water. Besides the five-star hotel complete with ballroom, restaurant, children's play area and exclusive bar, private apartments are also available in the hotel at the astronomical price of approximately $US 850,000 for 80 m^2 (= 860 square feet). However, even the most luxurious apartments cannot offer both a sea view and bright sunlight. The apartments facing north have the sea view, but have no direct sunlight. If you want a sunny apartment you have to do without the sea view. Even in this amazingly beautiful, and expensive place you can't have everything.

After we die we will live in a home that was designed by Jesus. What the Creator of the world can build is something that no earthly architect could even dream of. Jesus says, in John 14:2-3, "In my Father's house are many rooms; if it were not so, I would have told you. And if I go and prepare a place for you, I will come back and take you to be with me that you also may be where I am."

Jesus has been building our home for over two thousand years. How beautiful it must be! Any earthly comforts provided in the spa resort of Juist will be superseded by our home in heaven. If, in this Creation, even every snowflake and each acorn leaf is unique, then how much more will this be true of homes built by Jesus! There is no repetition; everything is especially tailored for the person who will reside there. We have a place in heaven for ever, under a sun that never sets.

H7: Heaven is a place where we shall reign

Heaven will be a place of singing and rejoicing for us, but we will also have duties: "And they will reign for ever and ever" (Rev 22:5).

In the Parable of the Ten Minas, described in Luke 19:11-27, each servant receives ten minas and is told to put this money to work. One servant increases the amount by ten, another by five. When Jesus judges, the first servant is told, "Well done, my good servant! ... Because you have been trustworthy in a very small matter, take charge of ten cities" (Luke 19:17). The second servant receives, in turn, what he deserves, "You take charge of five cities" (Luke 19:19).

We may conclude that, after we die, the responsibility of reigning will be handed over to us. The assigned areas will not be equal in size, but will depend on how hard we have worked for God's Kingdom here on earth. In heaven, we will reign together with Jesus. We have a part in the ruling in eternity.

Here, politicians do everything and anything to get elected. The position of governing will be handed to us in heaven. This task will involve many creative and changing duties. Completing our duties will be easy, for there will be no job stress, no ladder to climb, and no politics in heaven.

H8: Heaven is the place where Jesus is

Sometimes, historical meetings have wide-reaching consequences. For example, we owe the knowledge of how to make porcelain to the meeting of the physicist *Tschirnhaus* and the alchemist *Johann Friedrich Böttger*. Even today, something special can grow out of a surprise meeting, especially if God's hand is behind it. Two people who have never before met are brought together. They develop a common understanding about something and act accordingly, with significant consequences.

The one single meeting that has the most significant and wide-reaching consequences is when a person meets with God. That person then finds everlasting life in Jesus. The

Bible mentions many such meetings. Zacchaeus, the corrupt chief tax collector of Jericho, changed his way of life and became a believer (Luke 19:1-10). The finance officer of Ethiopia was looking for God in Jerusalem and found Him in the desert. Only after becoming secure in the knowledge of his salvation, does he go on his way, rejoicing (Acts 8:26-39). Saul became Paul through Jesus. Once a persecutor of Christians, Paul became the most important missionary of all time (Acts 26:12-18). In the same way, everyone can meet Jesus uniquely, if we approach Him with openness. Those who dare to meet Him are rewarded with entry into heaven.

Jesus prays to His Father in John 17:24, "Father, I want those you have given me to be with me where I am." This prayer is fulfilled in heaven. We will be with Him for all eternity. When faith is fully revealed it will be replaced by wonder. When the queen of Sheba arrived at the court of Solomon she cried in surprise, "Indeed, not even half… was told me" (2 Chron 9:6). This expression of surprise will be even more fitting when we arrive in God's kingdom. Here, on earth, there are still many pressing questions, to which we seek answers. There, with Jesus, everything will be explained: "In that day you will no longer ask me anything" (John 16:23).

"There will be no more night" in the presence of God and Jesus (Rev 22:5). We will no longer need sleep, therefore we will not need beds in heaven. The sun will shine forever. Yet it is not a celestial body which will provide the light. No created sun will shine for eternity, but "the glory of God gives it light, and the Lamb is its lamp [= Jesus]" (Rev 21:23). Isaiah saw the everlasting sun prophetically in God's kingdom: "The sun will no more be your light by day, nor will the brightness of the moon shine on you, for the LORD will be your everlasting light, and your God will be your glory. Your sun will never set again" (Is 60:19-20).

Thousands of people flock to overflowing beaches in their holidays to soak in the glowing sun most of them get nothing more than sunburn and have to live with the danger of skin cancer, worrying whether or not the SPF of their sunblock lotions is high enough to screen out harmful rays. However the everlasting sun of heaven will be good for us and will never burn. It will not be the scorching sun we know in the deserts of this earth (Rev 7:16).

H9: Heaven is where we become like Jesus

I hardly dare to say it, but it is written in 1 John 3:2: "Dear friends, now we are children of God, and what we will be has not yet been made known. But we know that when he appears, **we shall be like him**."

What does that mean? Man was created in the image of God, but this identity was lost in the Fall. The Bible is referring to Jesus when it says that, "the Son is the radiance of God's glory and the exact representation of his being" (Hebr 1:3). If in heaven we become like Jesus, then we too will be the radiance of God's glory and the exact representation of His being.

Individually, we will have our unique personalities, but our qualitative physical traits (beauty, glory, figure, physical perfection) will be that of Jesus (Phil 3:21). That body will not be restricted by time or space (John 20:19).

Here on earth, it is very rare that we meet someone who shares our thoughts and beliefs. But when this does happen, we cherish these conversations and time seems to fly. That which is said is stimulating and enriching, usually leading us to new discoveries which we would not have made but for the other person's input.

In heaven, we will become one in thought with Jesus. Communication with Him will be an integral creative element. Even after all of our earthly questions have been answered, there will still be new and boundless things to contemplate. Just like the way that those dear to us want to get to know us as well as possible, we will want to get to know the inexhaustible kingdom of God (Is 40:28) and Jesus (Col 2:3). Right after the creation of man, God gave him the creative task of naming the animals (Gen 2:19-20). Does it not follow that the Lord in heaven will continue this creative conversation? Communication in heaven is not an exchange of knowledge with which we could fill an encyclopedia, but a continually enriching dialogue.

H10:   Heaven is something special to look forward to

In looking at the content of Jesus' words, one aspect is impossible to ignore. He continually invited us to heaven. He began His preaching with the words, "the time has come. The kingdom of God is near. Repent and believe the good news" (Mark 1:15). Jesus tried to describe heaven to us in many parables. "The kingdom of heaven is like

- a man who sowed good seed in his field" (Matt 13:24).
- a mustard seed" (Matt 13:31).
- yeast" (Matt 13:33).
- treasure hidden in a field" (Matt 13:44).
- a merchant looking for fine pearls" (Matt 13:45).
- a net" (Matt 13:47).
- a king who prepared a wedding banquet for his son" (Matt 22:2).

The soul-searching conversation with Zacchaeus ends with a reference to eternal salvation: "Today salvation has come to this house. ... For the Son of Man came to seek and to save what is lost" (Luke 19:9-10).

Jesus does not promise children an easy life on this earth, but he promises them heaven: "Let the little children come to me, and do not hinder them, for the kingdom of God belongs to such as these" (Luke 18:16).

When Jesus sees the paralytic he does not tell him first "Get up and walk!", but "Your sins are forgiven" (Matt 9:2). It is once again clear that a decisive freedom from sin is a prerequisite for heaven and is of the utmost importance to Jesus.

The Sermon on the Mount is so often misquoted today, but heaven is its main subject:

- "Blessed are those who are persecuted because of right-eousness, for theirs is the kingdom of heaven" (Matt 5:10).
- "But seek first his kingdom and his righteousness and all these things will be given to you as well" (Matt 6:33).
- "Enter through the narrow gate. For wide is the gate and broad is the road that leads to destruction, and many enter through it. But small is the gate and narrow the road that leads to life, and only a few find it" (Matt 7:13-14).

As the disciples returned from a missionary journey, they rejoiced to know that even the demons submitted to them. Jesus reminded them that they had a much greater reason to rejoice, "Do not rejoice that the spirits submit to you, but rejoice that your names are written in heaven" (Luke 10:20). Jesus gives absolute priority to this particular reason for joy. 1 Peter 1:8 refers to this, saying: Rejoice "with an inexpressible and glorious joy."

If we show the way to glory to just one other person, it will result in insurmountable joy in heaven: "In the same way, I tell you, there is rejoicing in the presence of the angels of God over one sinner who repents" (Luke 15:10).

This means:

- The most important task God's children have is to spread the word that will lead people to heaven. This heavenly assignment still has utmost priority.

- Until the return of Jesus, the eternal goal must remain the main topic of biblical preaching and pastoral care.

- Knowing that we have a home in heaven (Phil 3:20) should form the substance of our lives and infect others with our joy.

APPENDIX

Annotations to the Bible

The following sections deal with the most important principles for understanding the Bible. The detailed subdivisions and the extensive numbering should make things easy to find.

I. Fundamental Principles of the Bible

In science it is customary to formulate the initial conditions necessary to gain knowledge in a specialized field in the form of established fundamental principles. The entire acquisition of knowledge is then based on this foundation. Even though this method cannot be transposed altogether to the Word of God because of the rather different nature of the Bible, we can, nevertheless (with that caveat in mind), compile the most essential principles. These principles are fundamental for dealing with the Bible and should be of particular help to those who have very little previous knowledge of it. This should make approaching the 'Book of Books' as easy as possible. The following basic principles each consist of a short statement, which is then substantiated and documented extensively by biblical quotes. There is a whole list of synonymous terms for the Bible (or parts thereof) which we also use: Word of Christ (Rom 10:17), Word of God (Matt 15:6), the Word of the Lord (1 Sam 15:23), Scroll of the Lord (Is 34:16), book (Jer 30:2), Scripture (Luke 4:21; Matt 21:42), Holy Scriptures (2 Tim 3:15), Old and New Testament (Covenant) (2 Cor 3:14 and Luke 22:20).

I.1 The Origin of the Bible

P10: *The Bible is the only written information revealed and authorized by God:* "This is what the LORD, the God of

Israel, says: 'Write in a book all the words I have spoken to you'." (Jer 30:2). As the exalted Lord, Jesus commands: "Write this down, for these words are trustworthy and true" (Rev 21:5). No words may be added to or taken away from the Bible (Deut 4:1-2; Rev 22:18-19) which is why all other books of so-called revelations (e.g. the Book of Mormon, the Qur'an of the Muslims) are not inspired by God. In Galatians 1:8 the uniqueness of biblical revelation is stressed as are the consequences of changing the gospel in any way: "But even if we or an angel from heaven should preach a gospel other than the one we preached to you, let him be eternally condemned!"

P11: *In the final analysis, man cannot fully grasp how the Bible came about* (Luke 1:1-4). It remains an unfathomable secret as to how the information was transferred from God to the writers of the Bible. The expressions "I [God] have put my words in your mouth" (Jer 1:9), "the word of the Lord came to me" (Ez 7:1) or "I [Paul] received it by revelation from Jesus Christ" (Gal 1:12) give us the distinct impression that, in reading the Bible, we are dealing with a divine source of information. However, just how the writers received the contents of the Bible, remains a mystery.

P12: *The divine aspect of the Bible:* God Himself is the source and originator of the Bible. According to 2 Timothy 3:16 all Scripture is God-breathed (Greek *theopneustos* = given by God and the Holy Spirit, breathed in by God). The source of the information is the triune God, the Father, the Son and the Holy Spirit:

a) *God, the Father:* "In the past God spoke to our forefathers through the prophets at many times and in various ways, but in these last days he has spoken to us by his Son, whom he appointed heir of all things, and through whom he made the universe" (Hebr 1:1-2).

b) *Jesus Christ:* "See to it that you do not refuse him [Jesus] who speaks. If they did not escape when they refused him who warned them on earth, how much less will we, if we turn away from him [Jesus] who warns us from heaven?" (Hebr 12:25).

c) *the Holy Spirit:* "But men spoke from God as they were carried along by the Holy Spirit" (2 Pet 1:21).

P13: *The human aspect of the Bible:* The Word of God is presented to us in earthen vessels, i.e. the divine thoughts about the mystery of God's ways, the incomprehensibility of His love and mercy are reproduced in the limited expressiveness of human language. Nevertheless the words are filled with "spirit and life" (John 6:63).

I.2   The Truth Content of the Bible

P20: *The word of the Bible is unswerving truth:* "Your word **is** truth" (John 17:17). The OT confirms this trait: "God is not a man, that he should lie, nor a son of man, that he should change his mind. Does he speak and then not act? Does he promise and not fulfil?" (Num 23:19). In John 14:6 Jesus testifies not only that He speaks the truth, but that He Himself is the truth personified. The German writer *Manfred Hausmann* (1898 – 1986) said with regard to the character of truth: "Truth is infinitely greater and deeper than mere rightness."

P21: *There is unity between Jesus and the Word of God:* Jesus Christ and the Word of God constitute an unfathomable unity (John 1:1-4; Rev 19:13). During His time on earth, Jesus was *true man* and *true God* at the same time. He is the Son of God and also the Son of Man. [He was] "made in human likeness. And being found in appearance as a man" (Phil 2:7-8), **but** in contrast to all other men He was without sin. In the same way the following applies to the Word of God: Externally, the Bible seems to be like other books; it is a book with many literary genres, **but** in contrast to all other books it is God's Word and as such is infallible, absolutely true (Ps 119:160) and completely flawless (Prov 30:5). P21 summarizes the principles P12 and P13.

P22: *There is no qualitative difference: The quality of truth does not change from biblical book to biblical book nor from writer to writer entrusted with the task:* So the OT cannot be played off against the NT (or vice versa) or the gospels against the letters written by Paul since all Scripture is based on revelation (Gal 1:12). However, the depth of meaning and relevance of these statements are by no means always the same. Thus the importance of the salvation account in John 3:16 cannot be compared to the journey detail of Acts 27:12, and the creation account according to Genesis 1 has a different ranking than the list of Jews returning to Israel as recorded in Ezra 2 (cp also Principle P50).

I.3 Testing Biblical Truths

P30: *Biblical truth can be tested to a certain extent:* God does not expect blind faith, instead He gives us convincing yardsticks against which to test His Word and thus help us to establish truth:

1. *Our lives:* Jesus teaches that the Word can be tested by applying it to our lives. "My teaching is not my own. It comes from him who sent me. If anyone chooses to do God's will, he will find out whether my teaching comes from God or whether I speak on my own" (John 7:16-17).

2. *Our freedom:* Jesus teaches that the application of a misleading system enslaves (ideologies and sect systems enslave man); the acceptance (and incorporation) of His thoughts into one's life, however, sets us free: "If you hold to my teaching, you are really my disciples. Then you will know the truth, and the truth will set you free" (John 8:31-32).

3. *By acceptance:* Just as the taste of an orange can only be experienced by tasting it, so the truth of the Bible can only become apparent to those who make an effort to get to know it and accept it. Discussions or arguments cannot replace intensive Bible study. The Bereans' actions were exemplary: "Now the Bereans were of more noble character than the Thessalonians, for they received the message with great eagerness and examined the Scriptures every day to see if what Paul said was true" (Acts 17:11).

4. *The results:* Positive growth will be evident in the life of everyone who lives in accordance with God's Word and takes heed of its admonitions (see also question QB2): "Do not let this Book of the Law depart from your mouth; meditate on it day and night, so that you may be careful to do everything written in it. Then you will be prosperous and successful" (Jos 1:8).

5. *Through preaching:* God has placed a special promise on listening to biblical preaching. Everyone who listens to the Word of God with an open heart, will believe: "Consequently, faith comes from hearing the message, and the message is heard through the word of Christ" (Rom 10:17).

6. *Our own sinful nature:* Perhaps more than any other Bible passages, those which refer to our sinful human nature authentically address the core of our being. Those honest with themselves will recognize the truth of the Bible in the personal diagnosis it gives us: "There is no difference, for all have sinned and fall short of the glory of God" (Rom 3:22-23). I doubt if there is anyone alive who would reject the words in 1 John 1:8 as not applying to them: "If we claim to be without sin, we deceive ourselves and the truth is not in us."

Note: It is remarkable that the truth of the Bible is understood only by those who act in obedience. Those who approach the Bible purely on an intellectual level, dissociated from their own person, find the Bible inaccessible (1 Cor 1:19). Thus, mathematically convincing calculations (see question QB1) can be helpful, but the step to faith remains an individual decision. The promises of God can only be accepted in faith or rejected in disbelief.

I.4 The Subject Matter of the Bible

P40: *The Bible speaks about Jesus:* This applies not only to the NT, since Jesus teaches also with regard to the OT: "You diligently study the Scriptures because you think that by them you possess eternal life. These are the Scriptures that testify *about me*" (John 5:39). We gain access to the OT by means of the NT because these Scriptures refer to Christ. Jesus taught this truth to the disciples on the road to Emmaus (Luke 24:13-35). This is the main objective of the Bible, which is stressed in John 20:31: It was "written that you may believe that Jesus is the Christ, the Son of God, and that by believing you may have life in his name."

P41: *The Bible speaks about things concerning this world and the next* (John 3:12). Things from this world are, for example, historical events, journey descriptions, personal happenings, laws, descriptions of moods, family chronicles, genealogies, missionary accounts, questions concerning everyday life and scientific data. Apart from these things (which God considers important, too) the Bible directs our eyes time and again toward heavenly things (Matt 6:33; Col 3:2): toward God, Jesus Christ and the Holy Spirit, toward the Kingdom of God, the resurrection and the Judgment, heaven and eternity.

P42: *The Bible portrays man most realistically:* The men and women of the Bible are not glorified as heroes, but described honestly with all their weaknesses and imperfections, their failures but also their exemplary actions. Even the failure of David, the "man after his [God's] own heart" is not covered up (2 Sam 11; Acts 13:22).

P43: *Biblical revelation is the key to understanding this world.* It is the fundamental source of information and it cannot be replaced by anything else: The present in particular cannot be explained if one ignores the three events of the past: *Creation, the Fall* and *the Flood*. Five sub-principles can therefore be deduced (explained in more detail in [G6]).

1. *The past is the key to the present.* This statement is in direct opposition to any fundamental statement made by the evolutionists, who say that we can extrapolate from today's observational data as far back as we want.

2. *The means of creation can only be understood by faith* (Hebr 11:3). The various means of creation are attested to by numerous scriptures:

- by the word of God: Ps 33:6; John 1:1-4; Hebr 11:3
- by the power of God: Jer 10:12
- by the wisdom of God: Ps 104:24; Prov 3:19; Col 2:3
- by the Son of God: John 1:1-4; John 1:10; Col 1:15-27; Hebr 1:2b
- by the very nature of Jesus : Matt 11:29; John 10:11; John 14:27
- without initial material: Hebr 11:3
- without using time: Ps 33:6

3. *Death is a result of the sin of the first people* (Gen 2:17; Gen 3:17-19; Rom 5:12; Rom 5:14; Rom 6:23; 1 Cor 15:21).

4. *Man's sin and its consequences have affected the entire visible* *creation* (Rom 8:20,22). The harmful structures in biology (e.g. bacteria causing illness; parasitism; killing mechanisms of snakes, spiders and animals of prey; carnivorous plants, troubles through "thorns and thistles") cannot be explained unless we take the Fall into account. The universally observable transcience and decay also have their cause here.

5. *The present geology of the earth cannot be explained without the Flood.*

I.5 Statements Made by the Bible

P50: *Not all biblical statements carry the same weight or have the same depth,* although there is no unimportant information. This becomes immediately apparent on comparing, for example, John 3:16 with Acts 18:1 (see Principle P22).

P51: *The Bible contains all the basic truths we need.* It is complete in the sense that it contains everything which is necessary in order to manage this life as well as to attain the eternal goal: "Look in the scroll of the LORD and read: None of these will be missing, not one will lack her mate" (Is 34:16).

P52: *The Bible does not contradict itself anywhere.* Apparent contradictions mostly dissolve on closer examination. The most frequent cause of such contradictions is that some biblical principles are ignored:

1. *The Bible's accounts are often very brief:* The conversion of Levi (= Matthew) is recounted in only one verse (Matt 9:9). Similarly, the question concerning the wives of Adam's sons finds its origin in the brevity of biblical accounts, which were obviously not intended to be exhaustive. According to Genesis 5:4 Adam fathered sons and *daughters*. Initially, then, brothers and sisters intermarried and in the following generation cousins intermarried. So soon after Creation, such close intermarriage posed no risk (see question QC 11).

2. *Some events in the Bible have parallel accounts concentrating on other aspects:*

Example 1: The genealogy of Jesus according to Matthew 1:1-17 and to Luke 3:28-38 show both correspondences and differences. In Matthew we find a typical descending line that begins with Abraham and ends with Joseph, Mary's husband. In Luke, however, we find a line of ascents that begins with Joseph and reaches back to Adam, even God. The genealogy in Matthew contains 3 x 14 names, that in Luke 77 names. This fact obviously has a symbolic meaning. For symbolic reasons, and to give a better overall view, both genealogies leave out names. However, they agree on the following statements:

- Jesus is not the son of Joseph
- Jesus is a "star out of Jacob" (Num 24:17)
- Jesus was from the tribe of Judah (Rev 5:5)
- Jesus is of royal descent through King David
  (1 Chron 28:4-7; Is 43:6; Rev 5:5)

Example 2: The various accounts of Jesus' Resurrection differ in minor details. This fact proves that the Gospels are eyewitness accounts and are not copies of one another. (When several eyewitnesses report about a traffic accident independently of one another, the descriptions are all somewhat different, even though all are true.)

3. *Some spiritual assertions reflect their true sense only when complemented.* The physics of light can only be described completely in a complementary (lat. *complementum* = something that completes or fills out) way: On the one hand, light behaves as a wave – on the other hand as a stream of material particles (photons). Only once these two behaviours which are actually contradictory are combined, can the real nature of light be understood. The Bible also contains such complementary statements. Thus, two seemingly contradictory statements, which are in reality complementary, are made about saving faith (see also question QS1):

a) "For we maintain that a man is justified by faith apart from observing the law" (Rom 3:28).
b) "You see that a person is justified by what he does and not by faith alone" (James 2:24).

4. *Some problems are due to the translation used.* Example: According to *Luther's* translation of the Bible Jacob buried the idols underneath an *oak tree* (Gen 35:4). The German Elberfeld translation stays closer to the original text and uses the original word "terebinth" (a turpentine tree).

Note: People do not reject the Bible because it contradicts itself but because it contradicts man.

5. *In isolated cases, the solution to ostensible contradictions is difficult yet possible in principle.* Examples for this are: the death of Judas (Matt 27:5b \ Acts 1:18), the contents of the ark of the covenant (1 Kings 8:9 \ Hebr 9:4), the death of Saul (1 Sam 31 \ 2 Sam 1).

Explanatory example: According to Matthew 27:5 Judas hanged himself. Different scriptures say: "He fell headlong, his body burst open and all his intestines spilled out" (Acts 1:18). These two statements concerning the death of Judas seem to contradict one another. They do, however, fit if one regards the latter statement, for example, as a very symbolic description; just as we would say: he was totally shattered, or if the branch or rope broke afterwards (see principle P59).

P53: *The Bible is the only book with true prophetic statements* which have been proved in space and time (see also question QB1).

Definition of prophecy: Prophecy is the certain forecast of a specific event in the future which cannot be arrived at through the normal means of human knowledge. Prophecy is thus the earlier announcement of later events, in contrast to historical recordings, which involve the subsequent announcement of earlier events. In John 13:19 Jesus refers to the faith strengthening intention of prophecy which precedes the event: "I am telling you now before it happens, so that when it does happen you will believe that I am He."

P54: *God often starts His revelations with a detail* which is later unfolded further, step by step. The most marked example for this way of proceeding are the prophecies concerning the coming of Christ into this world. [G1, pp.110-117]

P55: *When reading a text superficially, there is the danger that details are seen as unimportant trivia.* In the total context they usually have a deeper significance.

Example 1: The passage in Exodus 12:46 "Do not break any of the bones" refers to the passover, the lamb to be sacrificed. This is a prophetic sign for the "Lamb of God, who takes away the sin of the world" (John 1:29), Jesus. His bones likewise were not broken although it was Roman custom to break the legs of the crucified, as in the case of the two criminals next to Jesus (John 19:32-36).

Example 2: Jesus had to be crucified outside the city walls of Jerusalem as prophesied in the Old Testament because in those days, sacrificial animals were burnt outside the camp so as not to defile the people (Lev 16:27; Hebr 13:11-12).

P56: *Scripture contains messages of such depth that humans* *will never exhaust them fully* (1 Cor 13:12). The German theologian *Georg Huntemann* (1929 –) said: "What the Bible wants to tell us, commences beyond that which reason can explore."

P57: *The reach of biblical statements surpasses human thought.* The span of the Bible's time-frame is from "before the creation of the world" (Eph 1:4) right up to God's eternity (Rev 22:5). The Bible answers questions which no natural science can answer:

- What is the nature of death? Why does it exist and for how long will it exist?
- What is man? Where do we come from? What's the point of life and where are we going?
- What will eternity be like?

P58: The *Bible is a literary work in a class of its own*. Part of the literary wealth of the Bible is to present its message in such a variety of literary genres and styles as is not found in any other book:.

Poem (Ps 119), hymn (Col 1:15-17), love song (Song of Songs of Solomon), scientific account in everyday language (Genesis 1), historical account (Book of Ezra), allegory (situation taken from everyday life used as a comparison; Matt 13:3-23), parable (Greek *parabole* = set side by side; a special and singular situation is used as a teaching story to be interpreted comparatively, Luke 18:1-8), symbolic language (John 15:1), prophetic symbolic language (Rev 6), prophecy (Matt 24), paradox (Phil 2:12-13), sermon (Acts 17:22-31), warning (Col 3:16-17), praise (Eph 1:3), formula of blessing (Phil 4:7), teaching (Rom 5:12-21), family chronicle (1 Chr 3), prayer (Ps 35), personal testimony (1 John 1:1-2), recounting of dreams (Gen 37:6-7), God speaking directly (Matt 3:17), counselling (John 4:7-38), accounts of disputes (Acts 15:7-21) and trials (John 18:28-38), words of wisdom (Prov 13:7), promises (Mark 16:16), judgment (Matt 11:21-24), riddles (Judges 14:12-14), lawgiving (civil, criminal, moral, ritual, health), lyrical poetry (Song of Songs), biography (book of Nehemiah), personal correspondence (Paul's letter to Philemon), diary (Acts 16), monologue (Job 32-37), dialogue (Job 3-31), apocalyptic (Daniel, Revelation), temporal encoding (Daniel 12:9), prologue (Greek *prologos* = what is said before, Luke 1:1-4), epilogue (Greek *epilogos* = what is said afterwards; John 21:25), ellipsis (Greek *elleipsis* = what is left out, stylistic method of omitting unimportant detail, Matt 9:9), metaphor (Greek *metaphora* = transposition; symbolic expression used in a transposed sense, Obadiah 4), inscription (John 19:19), encoded message (Rev 13:18).

On the other hand the Bible does not contain: Saga, legends, myths, fairy tales, glosses, satires, comedy, jokes, utopianisms, science fiction. The literary modes of expression hyperbole (Greek *hyperballein* = go beyond the goal, exaggeration, Matt 11:18) and irony (Greek *eironeia* = dissemblance; 2 Cor 12:11) are used occasionally, where they are clearly recognizable as stylistic means.

No other book in world history has such a broad spectrum of genres while also being 100% truth from beginning to end.

P59: *The Bible exhausts the wealth of all literary forms.* As well as direct statements, which are used most often, numerous other specific forms of language are used in the Bible:

1. *Phenomenological language:* Instead of describing some phenomenon as it really happens, it is described as it is witnessed: Modern astronomy as well as the Bible speak about the sunrise and sunset although these phenomena are not produced by the movement of the sun, but by the rotation of the earth.

2. *Idiomatic expressions:* Short expressions are often more to the point than lengthy explanations (Judges 14:18 "If you had not plowed with my heifer").

3. *Poetic picturesque speech:* (Song of Songs 8:3): "His left arm is under my head and his right arm embraces me."

4. *Paraphrases and pictures for present-day jargon in science and technology:* The Bible describes technical achievements which did not even exist at the time of its writing, as well as situations for which modern science has invented terms: instead of satellites, space labs and orbital stations, the Bible describes in pictures: "Though you soar like the eagle and make your nest among the stars" (Ob 4). Instead of speaking about ontogenesis (embryonic development) in the uterus in gynaecological jargon the Bible describes the formation of the child in the mother's womb in a round-about way: "My frame was not hidden from you when I was made in the secret place. When I was woven together in the depths of the earth" (Ps 139:15).

5. *Scientifically factual formulation:* The creation account is a good example of this; thus for instance, in physically correct fashion, the method of time-measurement and the definition of the unit of time are named in succession (Gen 1:14,19).

6. *Pictures from everyday life to explain spiritual correlations:* Thus, the sower in the parable in Matthew 13:3-23 is the preacher of the biblical message, the seed is the Word of God, the thorns are obstacles and the good soil the open hearts of people.

P591: *Keeping in mind the literary genre* (Principle P58) *and type of language* (Principle P59) *each biblical passage has to be taken at face value.* Thus, the Bible's statements have to either be taken in their exact, straightforward, literal sense, or if another sense is clearly intended, true to that sense and precisely transposed.

a) literally: In Luke 24:44 Jesus teaches this way of dealing with the Scriptures: "This is what I told you while I was still with you: Everything must be fulfilled that is written about me in the Law of Moses, the Prophets and the Psalms." Other scriptures stress this way of proceeding, too: "And so was fulfilled what the Lord had said through the prophet" (Matt 2:15); "Today this scripture is fulfilled in your hearing" (Luke 4:21), "Have you never read in the Scriptures… ?" (Matt 21:42).

b) true to the sense and transposed precisely: When Jesus says "I am the vine, you are the branches" (John 15:5), then this cannot be taken literally but must be transposed true to its sense. The intended meaning is usually easily recognized, since picturesque speech is supposed to increase descriptiveness and facilitate understanding. In this case the core teaching is added at the end: "Apart from me you can do nothing."

I.6 The Value of Biblical Statements

P60: *The message of the Bible is the most precious information there is:* The evangelist *Wilhelm Pahls* (1936 –), well-known in Germany, rightly emphasizes: "The gospel is the best message ever told to mankind. Never has anything even remotely comparable been preached to man." In Psalm 119 the value of the Word of God, which surpasses all else, is praised repeatedly: "The law from your mouth is more precious to me than thousands of pieces of silver and gold" (verse 72), "I rejoice in your promise like one who finds great spoil" (verse 162).

P61: *Anyone who rejects the Word of God will be judged by it.* Just as the preaching of the Word of God leads to faith (Rom

10:17) and hence to salvation, the rejection and condemnation of it leads to ruin:

> 1 Samuel 15:23: "Because you have rejected the word of the LORD, he has rejected you as king".
> John 8:47: "He who belongs to God hears what God says. The reason you do not hear is that you do not belong to God."
> Acts 13:46: "We had to speak the word of God to you first. Since you reject it and do not consider yourselves worthy of eternal life, we now turn to the Gentiles."

P62: *The Bible consists of the Old and the New Testament.* Both sections are equally God's Word and cannot be played off against one another. The OT is often quoted in the NT. It is interesting to note that this rarely happens literally but that God combines this with a further step of revelation. In the NT, central Old Testament prophecies are fulfilled: "These [people of the OT] were all commended for their faith, yet none of them received what had been promised. God had planned something better for us" (Hebr 11:39-40). The Lord Jesus can be found even in the OT: "You diligently study the Scriptures because you think that by them you possess eternal life. These are the Scriptures that testify about me" (John 5:39).

P63: *The (Old Testament) Apocrypha* (Greek *apokryphos* = hidden, secret, unreal) *are not to be seen as God's Word.* They were written in the time between the OT and the NT. The most important objections to their equality with the Bible are:

1. They contain some teachings that contradict the Bible (breach of interpretation principle IP4, see Appendix Part II) such as forgiveness of sins by means of alms (Tob 12:9), advocation of magical practices (Tob 6:9), forgiveness of the deceased's sins by intercession of those left behind (2 Macc 12:46).

2. They were never part of the Jewish canon since they are later additions. The Apocrypha have therefore always been controversial. The dogma of the Catholic Church of the Council of Trent of 1546 ascribed equal value to the Apocrypha alongside the OT and the NT and must be viewed as a reaction to the Reformation.

3. They are not quoted by any writer of the NT although the NT refers to all but four short books of the OT.

4. The Apocrypha itself does not regard itself as faultless: In the prologue to the Book of Sirach (Ecclesiasticus) we read: "You are asked then to read with sympathetic attention, and make allowances if, in spite of all the devoted work I have put into the translation, some of the expressions appear inadequate".

Evaluation of the Apocrypha: Should one reject the Apocrypha altogether? *Luther* wrote the following, which he put at the beginning of these writings: "These are books, not of equal value to the Holy Bible, but which are still useful and profitable to read." The author of this book shares this opinion. If we do not ascribe the same importance to the Apocrypha as to the Bible, but read it in a poetic sense, as books of historical significance (such as Maccabees) we will still profit by it. The book of Sirach in particular is valuable since it comments on many possible situations in our daily life. It follows the Bible's books of wisdom with regard to content and form, while not claiming to be the Word of God.

I.7   Clarity and Understanding of the Bible

P70: *a) The Bible aims to be easily understood:* "For we do not write you anything you cannot read or understand" (2 Cor 1:13).

b) *At the same time, the Bible contains such profound ideas that we can never totally fathom them:* "For my thoughts are not your thoughts, neither are your ways my ways, declares the LORD. As the heavens are higher than the earth, so are my ways higher than your ways and my thoughts than your thoughts" (Is 55:8-9).

Charles H. Spurgeon (1834 – 1892) already referred to these two aspects [G1, p 94]: "The Bible contains great truths which surpass our understanding and show us how flat our limited intellect is. But the main and fundamental teachings of the Bible are not difficult to understand." The message of the Bible is accessible to everyone (Acts 17:11) yet its fullness and richness are inexhaustible (Rom 11:33).

P71: *The Bible was written under the guidance of the Holy Spirit by more than 45 authors entrusted with this task.* In the same way, its content cannot be correctly understood without the help of the Holy Spirit: "The man without the Spirit does not accept the things that come from the Spirit of God, for they are foolishness to him and he cannot understand them, because they are spiritually discerned. The spiritual man makes judgments about all things, but he himself is not subject to any man's judgment" (1 Cor 2:14-15).

I.8   The Accuracy of Biblical Statements

P80: *The Bible is incredibly accurate.* This trait becomes apparent when we examine it more closely with regard to its linguistic, semantic, spiritual, historical or scientific aspects.

The *persecution of Christians* exemplifies the accuracy of the historical aspect. At the beginning of church history the situation was still: "Men who have risked their lives for the name of our Lord *Jesus Christ*" (Acts 15:26) whereas regarding the end times, the Bible refers to "the souls of those who had been slain because of the *word of God* and the testimony they had maintained" (Rev 6:9). In our times, numerous beliefs have tried to integrate Jesus into their system. Islam has accepted Jesus as a prophet, the peace movement honours him as a pacifist, while others think him a good man and social reformer. For *Albert Schweitzer* (1875 – 1965) the historical Jesus was of interest. *Carl Friedrich v. Weizsäcker* (1912 – ; brother of the former German president) organized a peace council, suggesting that world peace can be accomplished by man. Many talk about Jesus, but only so long as He fits into their concept. The Muslim rejects Jesus as the Son of God. Only if we believe in Jesus, will "he himself [be] our peace" (Eph 2:14). Otherwise He is our judge (Acts 10:42), a fact which the Peace Movement conveniently ignores, along with the fact that it is Jesus who, as the Lamb in Revelation 6, opens the seal and sends the four apocalyptic riders as judgment in the shape of war and death. *Franz Alt* (1938 –), a well-known German writer, wrote a book about the Sermon on the Mount, but ignored the central command of Jesus to leave the broad path of damnation that leads to destruction and to enter through the narrow gate. Although Jesus is mentioned frequently, this is not enough. In the Sermon on the Mount Jesus warns:

> "Not everyone who says to me, 'Lord, Lord', will enter the kingdom of heaven, but only he who does the will of my Father who is in heaven. Many will say to me on that day, 'Lord, Lord, did we not prophesy in your name, … and perform many miracles?' Then I will tell them plainly, 'I never knew you. Away from me, you evildoers!' " (Matt 7:21-23).

Those that only stress Jesus' human side, never offend. But we have to preach the Jesus the Bible talks about (John 7:38). Many are offended when Jesus is presented as the Son of God.

At a time when standards are crumbling, persecution awaits those who accept the whole message of the Bible and stand for the "it is written" – be that by accepting the entire creation account or the biblical Jesus. Standing up for the Word of God and witnessing carries the promise of victory (Rev 12:11). Further examples are given in [G1, pp. 102-110].

I.9 The Timeframe of Biblical Statements

P90: *The Word of God is timeless.* Isaiah contrasts the transience of plants and the immortality of the Word of God: "The grass withers and the flowers fall, but the word of our God stands for ever" (Is 40:8), and Jesus compares the transient stars with His Word: "Heaven and earth will pass away, but my words will never pass away" (Matt 24:35). *Martin Luther* (1483 – 1546) said: "The Bible is neither antique nor modern, it is everlasting." The Bible transcends time, since its concepts and perspectives on behaviour apply beyond the actual time in which it was written. Although abortion, gene technology and drug abuse are not mentioned, the Bible gives clear indications as to what attitude to take. No other book is of such depth of penetration. Thus, for example, our human system of justice has no jurisdiction if there are no laws governing some new field.

I.10 The Accessibility of the Bible: Turning to Jesus Christ

After all that has been said, we must now ask how we can get access to the Bible. How can the uninitiated read and understand the Bible? After an evangelistic meeting a young intellectual came for counselling, honestly wanting to understand the Bible. In the course of our conversation I managed to help him overcome several of his objections and he replied

that he would now read the Bible in the light of the philosophical thought trends with which he was familiar. I replied:
"You can do that, but then you will not find the living God
who revealed Himself through Christ, but the impersonal,
pantheistic God of the philosophers. Philosophers have read
the Bible from within the framework of their own thinking,
but they did not find the God who becomes our salvation
only through Jesus. You can have access to the Bible and
to the living God tonight if you give your life to Him. Do
you want to do that?" The young man stayed and took the
advice I offered.

At this point I would like to outline my part in that conversation, using this one case as an example to show the reader the
way to faith in Jesus.

P100: *Recognize yourself:* Let us read Romans 3:21 together:
"There is no difference, for all have sinned and fall short
of the glory of God" (Rom 3:22-23). This scripture shows
us that we are lost in the sight of the living God; we cannot
come to Him because sin separates us from Him and we
possess nothing which commends us to Him. In brief: we
lack all merit before God. Since the Fall, there is a chasm
between the living God and sinful mankind. Do you agree
with God's diagnosis?

P101: *The only way out:* There is only one way out of this di-
lemma, and it is entirely God's doing. His Son was punished on
the cross for our sins. Jesus came to save what was lost (Matt
18:11). Salvation is found in no one else (Acts 4:12). Can you
accept this fact as well?

P102: *Confess your sins:* We will read 1 John 1:8-9: "If we
claim to be without sin, we deceive ourselves and the truth
is not in us. If we confess our sins, he is faithful and just and
will forgive us our sins and purify us from all unrighteous-

ness." Jesus has the authority to forgive sin. If we trust in His promise and confess our sin to Him and ask His forgiveness, we can be assured of His faithfulness. We can rely on the fact that He will truly set us free from the burden of our sin and its eternal consequences. But thinking about this is not enough. You have to act! Are you willing to do that? Let us now tell the Lord Jesus all this in prayer (this is the basis for a freely formulated prayer):

> "Lord Jesus, I have heard about You today and I understand why You came into this world. In your boundless love you have also taken hold of me. You see all my sin – that which is revealed to me now and also that which is as yet hidden from me. You, however, know all things, every culpable deed, every wrong stirring of my heart, You have recorded everything. I am an open book to You; the way my life is, I cannot stand before you. So I ask You now: Forgive all my sin and cleanse me thoroughly. Amen."

We have told the Lord everything that is necessary for now (1 John 1:8-9). God Himself vouches for His promise. How much of your guilt do you think He has forgiven? 80%? 50%? 10%? It is written: "[He] purif[ies] us from **all** unrighteousness" (1 John 1:9). You have been forgiven **completely**! Yes, all of it, 100%! This is fact, not just an assumption, a possibility or a hope! The Bible is adamant about this, we must be certain of this fact. Let us read 1 Peter 1:18-19 and 1 John 5:13 in this context.

P103: *Surrendering your life:* The Lord Jesus has forgiven all your sin. Now you can entrust your whole life to Him. In John 1:12 we read: "Yet to all who received him, to those who believed in his name, he gave the right to become children of God." All those who invite the Lord Jesus to take over the control of their lives receive the authorization to become children of God. Becoming God's children is not a reward we receive for any of our good deeds or because we are pious or because we go to a particular church. We become children of God if we have entrusted our lives to the Son of God and are willing to follow Him in obedience. Let us affirm this in a prayer:

> "Lord Jesus, You have forgiven all of my sin. I can hardly grasp this yet, but I trust in Your promise. And now I ask You to enter my life. Lead me and guide me on the way that You show me. I know that You want the best for me and so I want to entrust every area of my life to You. Let me get rid of everything that is not right before You. Give me new habits with You, which are under Your blessing. And give me an obedient heart so that I will do what Your Word says. Help me not to pay attention to various influences and all manner of human opinions, but open up Your Bible to me so that I might understand Your Word correctly and live accordingly. You shall be my Lord, and I want to follow You. Amen."

P104: *Accepted:* The Lord has accepted you! He has bought you at great cost to Himself, He saved you. You are now a child of God. A child is also an heir: heir of God, heir to the heavenly world. Can you imagine what is taking place in heaven right now? "… maybe joy?" Certainly! In Luke 15:10 we read: "There is rejoicing in the presence of the angels of God over one sinner who repents." Your conversion gives rise to great joy in heaven. All of heaven is involved when *one* person takes the message of the gospel seriously and accepts it into their life. The Bible calls this process of turning to Jesus *conversion*; we give Him our guilt and He removes it. At this point in time we become born again: He gives us new life. Now we are His children. Conversion and rebirth belong together. They are the two sides of one and the same coin.

P105: *Thanksgiving:* Salvation is God's gift to us. Only through His love has this path of salvation been made possible. We cannot contribute anything to this act of redemption. Everyone who receives a gift, says "Thank you!" Let us do that now. Formulate in your own words a prayer of thanks. Tell the Lord Jesus now: ...

P106: What now? The Bible compares the state you are now in to that of a newborn child. As a newborn child clearly belongs to its family, you also belong to God's family. Newborn children find themselves in a critical phase of life which is characterized by infant mortality. This phenomenon is present concerning our faith, too. Through conversion, the child is born. There is new life. Now nourishment, care and attention are absolutely necessary for this child. God has made provisions and has done everything so that you can develop in the right direction. The death of our infant faith can be avoided if we follow God's advice. The following aspects are not only important for a life as disciple to Jesus, they are indispensable prerequisites for everyday life with Jesus. If we adhere to these five points, we have God's guarantees that we will reach our designated goal:

1. God's Word

You have made your decision based on God's Word, the Bible. The Bible is the only book authorized by God. No other book equals the Bible in authority, truth, amount of information and origin. Reading God's Word is absolutely necessary to nourish your new life. In 1 Peter 2:2, this aspect is emphasized and clearly expressed: "Like newborn babies, crave pure spiritual milk." Make time each day to read the Bible in order to get to know about God's will. Preferably, start by reading one of the Gospels (for example, the Gospel of John). Let reading the Bible become a pleasant and everyday habit. You never forget to have breakfast and brush your teeth. Be as consequent in reading the Bible and make it an essential part of your day.

2. Prayer

Speak with God every day. He speaks *to us* through His Word, and He wants us to speak *to Him*. It is a great privilege to tell Him everything. According to the Bible, prayer can only be to God who is now your Father and to Jesus, your Saviour, your Good Shepherd, your friend – your everything. The Bible does not tell us to direct our prayers to anyone else. Prayer will give you strength. It will change you in a positive manner. Everything in your daily life can become a subject for prayer: your sorrows, pleasures, plans. Thank the Lord for all that you find moving. Pray for other people and their difficulties. Pray to the Lord that the people surrounding you will also find faith. Prayer and reading God's Word trigger a "spiritual circulation" which is necessary for a healthy spiritual life.

3. Obedience

When reading the Bible you will find many useful instructions on all areas of life and how to live with God. Translate all that you have understood into action and you will be blessed by the Lord. God takes pleasure in us being obedient children who live according to His Word and heed His commands. The best way to show our love for the Lord is by obeying Him: "This is love for God: to obey his commands" (1 John 5:3). This world offers different paths but the Bible sets a standard which is blessed by the Lord: "We must obey God rather than men!" (Acts 5:29).

4. Fellowship

God created mankind with a need for fellowship. Thus, you should look for other Christians who have surrendered their life to God, and keep in touch with them. These are the people with whom you can pray and talk about your faith. If a glowing coal is taken out of a fire, it will soon grow cold. As a rule, our love for Jesus will also grow cold if it is not kept alive through fellowship with other believers. Join a Bible believing church and take an active part in this community. A good evangelical church where people believe in the whole Bible is so important for our Christian walk. Don't neglect fellowship!

5. Faith

After our conversion and rebirth it is important that we continue to grow spiritually. Paul wrote to Timothy: "But as for you, continue in what you have learned" (2 Tim 3:14). At the end of his life Paul could say: "I have fought the good fight, I have finished the race, I have kept the faith" (2 Tim 4:7). Let us follow his example and remain faithful, too.

Conversion is not an end, but the beginning of a new life. You are now able to be God's co-worker (1 Cor 3:9). Help to ensure that others might also experience salvation in Jesus. Conversion has two consequences: firstly, our earthly life takes on a whole new meaning and secondly, we become God's children, heirs to eternal life.

Let us note: We cannot gain access to the Bible if we remain neutral observers. We have to become 'insiders'. A person who has surrendered his or her life to God in Jesus Christ in conversion, and experienced salvation, is such an insider, having 'boarded the lifeboat'. Individual spiritual counselling differs from case to case. The above conversation, however, reconstructs the most essential aspects of a conversion: we need to recognise our sinfulness, admit our sin, and surrender to Jesus Christ. This is where the process of spiritual growth begins.

I.11 Conclusion

We have tried to summarize the most important aspects of the Bible in the form of some fundamental principles. Such a human endeavour regarding a divine book can never be complete, and will certainly never suffice to adequately describe the riches of the Bible.

II.   Principles for Interpreting the Bible

IP1: *The Bible is self-explanatory.* In other words: There is no better commentary on the Bible than the Bible itself. This important principle is practised constantly by Jesus (e.g. Matt 19:3-6), the apostles (e.g. Gal 3:16) and the prophets of the Bible.

IP2: *Jesus Himself is the key to all interpretation.* Thus, the OT in particular remains incomprehensible without reference to Jesus (e.g. Ps 110:1; Is 53).

IP3: *The interpretation must not contradict other scriptures* (see also principle P52).

IP4: *No important teaching should be deduced from a single sentence or verse.* Important central messages are repeated in various contexts or formulated differently.

Examples:
- the sinlessness of Jesus (1 John 3:5; 1 Pet 2:22; 2 Cor 5:21)
- the sinfulness of man (Gen 8:21; Ps 14:2-3; Is 1:5-6; Matt 15:19; Rom 3:23)
- God's plan of salvation (Ez 34:12; Matt 9:13; 1 Thess 5:9; 1 Tim 2:4)

Note: The observation that Jesus loves the Father (John 14:31) and that the Father loves us (John 16:27) only appears once in explicit form in the Bible. However, this fact is implicit or assumed in a multitude of other statements, and so we may safely expound this as a scriptural teaching.

IP5: *Always consider the context and the overall consensus of the Bible.* Ignoring this principle has led to false teaching and harmful sects. Cross-references are of particular value.

IP6: *Some biblical doctrines can be deduced from the totality of similar individual events.* The Bible is no dull law- or text-book . In thousands of examples it shows us how or how not to interact with God and our fellow men. If we examine the common factor in different accounts dealing with similar topics, then we should be able to deduce a biblical teaching. A fitting example for this is the detailed description of the history of Israel: God's blessings or judgment on this nation (1 Cor 10:11). Question QL6 was answered by using this principle of interpretation.

IP7: *The OT is the indispensable decoder for the NT*, i.e. without the OT many parts of the NT remain obscure (e.g. Creation, the Fall, the Flood).

IP8: *The NT has a broader revelational spectrum than the OT.* This is verified by examining the letter to the Hebrews. Let us explain IP8 by talking about revenge. It is part of human nature to feel vengeful if we have been injured, to want the person harming us to "pay dearly", often in excess of the original damage: "If Cain is avenged seven times, then Lamech seventy-seven times" (Gen 4:24). In the Laws given on Mount Sinai God drastically restricts revenge to "one for one": *one* eye \ *one* eye; *one* tooth \ *one* tooth; *one* wound \ *one* wound; *one* bruise \ *one* bruise (Ex 21:24-25). In the Sermon on the Mount, Jesus intensifies the Old Testament law, introducing each instance with the six-fold expression "but I tell you." Applying Deuteronomy 32:35 to Exodus 21:24-25 he forbids any revenge: "But I tell you, do not resist an evil person. If someone strikes you on the right cheek, turn to him the other also" (Matt 5:39).

IP9: *Sin is not condoned anywhere in the Bible* even if it is not condemned in each particular passage. This principle is of special importance for the interpretation of the parable of the shrewd manager according to Luke 16:1-8 (see [G7]).

IP10: *"Do not go beyond what is written"* (1 Cor 4:6).

IP11: *Biblical truth always has priority over any other source of wisdom* provided the Bible has something to say on that specific subject. "See to it that no-one takes you captive through hollow and deceptive philosophy, which depends on human tradition and the basic principles of this world rather than on Christ" (Col 2:8).

IP12: *It is important to exhaust all textual subtleties (grammatical and semantic).* In Galatians 3:16 Paul uses Genesis 22:18 to show how to interpret the Scriptures.

IP13: *There are reasonably accurate translations (King James, NIV, Revised Standard) and less exact ones (e.g. Good News, Living Bible).* If in doubt, go back to the original text (Hebrew for the OT and Greek for the NT). The basic meaning of a particular word is often revealed by looking at several other contextual passages where the word's usage is more easily understood. Different translations have different objectives. The German translation by *Martin Luther*, for example, is characterized by its pithy and choice language. Utmost caution is advised when using translations where the translator has included his own comments. "Bibles" which consciously depart from the original text and harmonize with the teachings of a specific sect must be rejected (e.g. New World translation of the Jehovah's Witnesses).

IP14: *Some apparently contradictory passages of the Bible are actually complementary* (cp. in this context principle P52, point 3).

III. Why Read the Bible?

God wills that reading the Bible should be – like eating and drinking – one of life's daily necessities. This why we read in Jeremiah 15:16a: "When your words came, I ate them." The Bible itself lists numerous reasons as to why we should not forget to read it. The most important are set out below:

1. *to come to know the nature of God:* The nature of God – His greatness (Ps 19), His love (1 John 4:16), His mercy (Num 14:18), His faithfulness (Ps 25:10), His truth (Num 23:19) – is revealed through His word.

2. *for faith:* "Faith comes from hearing the message, and the message is heard through the word of Christ" (Rom 10:17).

3. *for spiritual growth:* "Like newborn babies, crave pure spiritual milk, so that by it you may grow up in your salvation" (1 Pet 2:2).

4. *for assurance of salvation:* "I write these things to you who believe in the name of the Son of God so that you may know that you have eternal life" (1 John 5:13).

5. *for correct teaching:* " … the trustworthy message as it has been taught, so that he can encourage others by sound doctrine and refute those who oppose it" (Titus 1:9). The Bible provides us with the necessary correction for our thinking and living. The sectarian, however, uses the Bible as a reference work to find confirmation of things he has been indoctrinated with.

6. *for safe passage through life:* "Your word is a lamp to my feet" (Ps 119:105).

7. *for setting priorities in life:* "But seek first his kingdom and his righteousness, and all these things will be given to you as well" (Matt 6:33).

8. *for guidelines on bringing up our children:* "Fix these words of mine in your hearts and minds; ... Teach them to your children" (Deut 11:18-19).

9. *for proper conduct with one's neighbour:* "Love your neighbour as yourself" (Matt 19:19), "but in humility consider others better than yourselves" (Phil 2:3). "Love your enemies, bless those who curse you, do good to those who hate you and pray for those who persecute you" (Matt 5:43).

10. *for joy and refreshment:* " ... for by them you have renewed my life" (Ps 119:93b). "[Your words] were my joy and my heart's delight" (Jer 15:16).

11. *for comfort in testing situations:* "I am laid low in the dust; renew my life according to your word" (Ps 119:25).

12. *for help in trouble:* "And call upon me in the day of trouble; I will deliver you, and you will honour me" (Ps 50:15).

13. *for protection from going astray:* "I gain understanding from your precepts; therefore I hate every wrong path" (Ps 119:104). Jesus makes ignorance responsible for people going astrray: "You are in error because you do not know the Scriptures or the power of God" (Matt 22:29).

14. *for protection against sinning:* "I have hidden your word in my heart that I might not sin against you" (Ps 119:11).

15. *for the confession of sin:* "All Scripture is ... useful for teaching, rebuking, correcting and training in righteousness" (2 Tim 3:16).

16. *for the interpretation of the times:* "The revelation of Jesus Christ … to show his servants what must soon take place" (Rev 1.1).

17. *as the basis for scientific works:* The Bible supplies us with basic principles for numerous sciences. These working prerequisites are indispensable in particular in fields involving questions of origin (e.g. cosmology, geology, biology) or where our view of man plays an important role (e.g. psychology, medicine).

18. *to recognize the will of God:* "… Then you will be able to test and approve what God's will is" (Rom 12:2). The will of God has been made clear not only in the Ten Commandments (Ex 20:1-17) but also in various other passages in the Bible (e.g. 1 Thess 4:3; 1 Thess 5:18; 1 Pet 2:15; Hebr 10:36; Hebr 13:21).

19. *for the cleansing of one's mind:* "You are already clean because of the word I have spoken to you" (John 15:3).

20. *to know how to act wisely:* "The fear of the LORD is the beginning of wisdom; all who follow his precepts have good understanding" (Ps 111:10).

IV. How Should We Read the Bible?

R1: We should read the Bible with an *attitude of prayer*. *Luther* gives us the wise advice: "Do not place your hand on the Scriptures but rather follow its footsteps adoringly".

1. *asking for understanding:* "Open my eyes that I may see wonderful things in your law" (Ps 119:18).
2. *giving thanks and praising God:* "May my lips overflow with praise, for you teach me your decrees" (Ps 119:171).

3. *as someone who has received a great gift:* "I rejoice in your promise like one who finds great spoil" (Ps 119:162).

R2: We should read the Bible *expectantly*: "I open my mouth and pant, longing for your commands" (Ps.119:131).

R3: We should read the Bible *spiritually*: " … we serve in the new way of the Spirit, and not in the old way of the written code" (Rom 7:6). Although the Bible commands us to be accurate when dealing with the Scriptures (see principle P80), it also warns us against the legalism of a frozen and lifeless faith (Matt 23:23,33). The Bible calls our attention to the Spirit: "He [God] has made us competent as ministers of a new covenant – not of the letter but of the Spirit; for the letter kills, but the Spirit gives life" (2 Cor 3:6).

R4: We should read the Bible *humbly*. God's thoughts are higher than our minds which is why we should not doubt even if there are things we do not understand. This takes humility: "'For my thoughts are not your thoughts, neither are your ways my ways,' declares the LORD" (Is 55:8).

R5: We should read the Bible *lovingly*. "Oh, how I love your law!" (Ps 119:97).

R6: We should read the Bible *trustingly*: "But because you say so, I will let down the nets" (Luke 5:5).

R7: We should read the Bible as a *personal letter* from God to us, a love letter [G1, pp. 186-188]. To quote *A. Bengel*, a well-known Christian theologian: "The Scriptures are a letter which God wrote to me, according to which I should live and according to which my God will judge me."

R8: We should read the Bible *frequently*: "Let the word of Christ dwell in you richly as you teach and admonish one another with

all wisdom, and as you sing psalms, hymns and spiritual songs
with gratitude in your hearts to God" (Col 3:16).

V. Ten Promises for Those who Read the Bible (Readers and Doers of the Word)

Promise 1: *Belonging to God:* "He who belongs to God hears
what God says" (John 8:47).

Promise 2: *Peace:* "Great peace have they who love your law,
and nothing can make them stumble" (Ps 119:165).

Promise 3: *Joy:* "I have told you this so that my joy may be in
you and that your joy may be complete" (John 15:11).

Promise 4: *Blessing:* "Blessed is he who keeps the words of the
prophecy in this book" (Rev 22:7).

Promise 5: *Fruitfulness:* "He is like a tree planted by streams
of water, which yields its fruit in season and whose leaf does
not wither. Whatever he does prospers" (Ps 1:3).

Promise 6: *Success:* "Do not let this Book of the Law depart
from you mouth; meditate on it day and night, so that you
may be careful to do everything written in it. Then you will
be prosperous and successful" (Jos 1:8).

Promise 7: *Answers to prayer:* "If you remain in me and my
words remain in you, ask whatever you wish, and it will be
given you" (John 15:7).

Promise 8: *Cleansing of one's thoughts:* "You are already clean
because of the word I have spoken to you" (John 15:3).

Promise 9: *Wisdom:* " ... the holy Scriptures, which are able to make you wise for salvation through faith in Christ Jesus" (2 Tim 3:15). "If any of you lacks wisdom, he should ask God… and it will be given to him" (James 1:5).

Promise 10: *Gift of eternal life:* "Whoever hears my word and believes him who sent me has eternal life and will not be condemned; he has crossed over from death to life" (John 5:24).

An Unabridged Reader's Letter

It's July of 1987, about half past seven on a Friday night. Here I am, from Düsseldorf, strolling through the shopping mall in Munich towards the Marienplatz. In front of a fashion house, someone hands me a piece of paper. It's an invitation to hear some professor talk about "Why do stars exist?" in the *Mühlhäuser* fashion house in a few minutes time. "Interesting topic," I thought, "but he wouldn't know that any more than I would. I may as well hear what he has to say."

Dear Mr. *Gitt*,

Today I know, that was it! I remember that your lecture was strongly attacked at the time by some people who, like me, had walked in off the street. However, I still know that I just kept thinking, what are on about? Can't they see that this man is speaking the truth ? How can they be so blind? He's absolutely right!"

Until then, I didn't want to have anything to do with faith, the church or anything like that. For me, Jesus was a person just like anybody else. Despite this, your talk led me to make the most important decision of my life. On the following (and last) evening of your lectures, I gave my life to the Lord Jesus. Dear Mr. *Gitt*, you were the worker for God's Kingdom who led me to make that decision. Today, ten years later, I want to express my gratitude to you!

I was twenty-nine then. Nine months after your lectures, I was baptised in a Baptist church in Düsseldorf. However, in the time that followed my life got into a bad way. I was not a source of joy for my heavenly Father. On the contrary: I went astray, grew attached to worldly things, and lived in opposition to God's Word.

Today I know that it was out of grace that the Lord Jesus held me and put me on to the right path. I would like to give an example of how this happened, once again with your help:
Without havin any special destination in mind, my wife and I went on a short break in Holland. We arrived in the coastal town of Noordwijk. It was out of season and there was plenty of accommodation to choose from. We chose one of the many guest houses on the main street, and went to our room. There was some literature laid out for the guests: a book and the magazine 'ethos'. I opened the book and read the first few sentences of the preface:

"The idea for this book originated during a number of evangelistic talks which the author held in the somewhat novel surroundings of the *Mühlhäuser* fashion house in Munich. Every night for a week, the couturier *Harro Mühlhäuser* allowed us to use the first floor of his business premises ..." (see Preface).

Bang! It really hit me! You just can't imagine what was going on inside me! The man who had led me to the Lord Jesus was speaking to me again! And how he spoke! The answers in this 'Questions' book were exactly fitting for the state that my faith was in at the time.

That was in the spring of 1993. Today, ten years after your evening lectures in Munich, I am thirty-nine years old, my wife is a Christian, and we have three children, aged four, two and almost one. Then, my life lacked meaning. I had no sensible outlook on life. Today I have the right outlook on life and what a difference it makes! I have found the meaning of life, namely being a child of the living God through faith in our mutual Lord Jesus. I trust in God's Word, stand firm in the faith and have found my place in the congregation. I have found the way, the truth and the life.

Dear Mr. *Gitt*, thank you very much!

Dietmar Schmidt
Grevenbroich, 24th July 1997

The Author: A Personal Profile

What follows, is an account of how the Lord found me through Jesus Christ. By recounting a few episodes from my life with the Lord I'd like to show how He has worked, called, guided and been a blessing in my life.

1. Childhood and Adolescence: I was born on 22 February 1937 on my parents' farm in Raineck/Ebenrode, East Prussia. Until our flight as refugees, I had a happy and untroubled childhood in these rural surroundings. In October 1944, when I was 7 and just in the second year at school, we had to flee with our horse and carriage from Raineck to Peterswalde (southern East Prussia). The news about the Russian invasion reached us in January 1945, far too late. The curt official announcement was bound to cause panic: "Save yourselves, those who can". Since I was ill and had a high temperature, they just carried my bed from the lounge and loaded me onto the refugee wagon. Once again, a trek with horse and carriage hurriedly got under way but we were soon stopped by the Russians. My brother Fritz, then 15 years old, was abducted. He never returned. My mother (*Emma Gitt*, née *Girod*) was deported to the Ukraine soon afterwards and died not long after that. Two of my aunts, my cousin *Rena*, my grandfather and I were expelled by the Poles in November 1945. My grandfather died of exposure after a night without shelter even before the 10-day transport by cattle train from Osterode/East Prussia got under way. After a stop-over in Sanitz close to Rostock, we finally reached the town of Wyk on the North Sea island of Föhr.

My father was a Prisoner of War in France and knew nothing of what had happened to his family. Unlike his fellow prisoners, he could not write letters, using the sheets of writing paper which were distributed on a monthly basis, since nearly all our relatives came from East Prussia. He did not know the whereabouts of those of his relatives who had had to flee. One night at camp, he dreamt about a distant relative who had lived in the Rhineland before the war. In this dream they talked for the first time in years. As they parted, the relative said, "*Hermann*, do come and visit me." My father answered in his dream: "But where do you live? I do not know your address." The relative replied "Bochum, Dorstener Street 134a." My father woke up, lit a candle in the middle of the night and wrote down the address revealed to him in the dream. He told this strange dream to his friends in the dormitory. They laughed at him, because he took the whole thing so seriously, saying that he would write the following day. The reply he received confirmed this address to be absolutely correct and he was thus able to contact my aunt (*Lina Riek*, née *Girod*) in Wyk on the island of Föhr via this distant uncle. The news that my father was alive made me very happy. I could hardly believe that I was not an orphan after all but that I had a father again. When my father returned from French captivity in 1947, he found me as sole survivor of his lost family. His search for work led us to a farm in Saaße in Northern Germany.

What stands out in my mind about that time is that some boys from the village invited me to a *children's hour*. I could not imagine what a children's hour might be and thought that they would tell fairy tales. So I went along and experienced the first of many hours spent in the only room of the community nursing sister who worked in that village. With great charisma, Sister *Erna* told us Bible stories every Sunday morning. She prayed and sang lots of songs, praising God with us. After the very first hour I knew this had nothing to do with fairy tales. I was touched by the message. What I heard really spoke to me and I began to attend these meetings regularly.

My father remarried the following year and I soon moved in with his new wife in the nearby village of Jeetzel, while my father worked on the land several villages further on. My stepmother (*Adelheit Gitt*, née *Lipowski*) became very fond of me. She had to work hard as a seamstress for the local farmers, struggling to make do with the little she could earn in addition to free board. She was a practising Catholic, but she never tried to persuade me to convert to Catholicism during this susceptible age and I still think highly of her for that. I continued to go to the children's hour regularly, come rain or shine. The faithful ministry of Sister *Erna* sowed the seed of God's Word in my heart which would later germinate. When my father found a job in industry in Westphalia in 1950, we moved to Hohenlimburg. Unfortunately, I was not to find such encouraging fellowship. In fact, the opposite was the case. The religious instruction in school had such a liberal, Bible-critical orientation that it caused me to look back on the children's hour and think: "A pity that those Bible stories which Sister *Erna* told us are not true after all." But the smouldering wick, the yearning for truth, was never completely extinguished. And the occasional church visit was no help in my search for God, either. The sermons were usually very non-committal and did not call people to a change of heart.

2. My Way to God: I finished my degree in Hannover, and after doing my Ph.D. in Aachen, I started as head of what is now Information Technology at the Federal Institute of Physics and Technology (Physikalisch-Technische Bundesanstalt, PTB) in Brunswick in October 1971. My situation then can be summed up as follows: I had been successful professionally. I had passed the degree examination in two specialized fields effortlessly with *cum laude* and my doctorate with distinction; I also received the *Borchers* medal from the University of Aachen. I was immediately offered a leading position as a scientist. In 1966 I got married. We had two children and were a happy family. We were well off all round, and we had no family problems; we were all healthy and had no money worries. One might have thought we had no need for God in our lives. I stress this because I often hear testimonies of people who only opened up to the gospel because of a particular personal problem. This was not so in my case since God's ways with the individual are as diverse as there are people on this earth.

In the autumn of 1972 my wife and I attended two very different evangelistic meetings that took place in Brunswick. A small Christian group was responsible for one set of meetings, at the secondary school in our residential area. They handed out a Bible and a red pen to every visitor and I thought this was a very good idea. The congregation was actively involved in studying central scriptures and we underlined all the scriptures we dealt with. On completion of this unusual but very effective week of preaching, we could keep the Bibles. Thus, my wife and I both had our own identical Bible and when reading, we often came across passages marked in red, making us feel at home. The other campaign took place shortly afterwards. Every day approximately 2000 people came to the City Hall in Brunswick. The topics were taken from a narrow spectrum of messages, all unequivocally calling for a decision. The call to a life of faith, a commitment to Jesus Christ was made every night; the invitation was clear. After a sermon by *Leo Janz* on Luke 17:33-36, the choice between salvation and damnation became so clear, that I overcame my fear and trembling and responded to the invitation to come forward. My wife went forward, too. Individual talks and prayer with counsellors made us sure of our salvation. Interestingly enough, both of the people we spoke to belonged to the home Bible study group which we joined later on. More evangelistic evenings in Brunswick followed. Some nights at the Martini Church, when Pastor *Heinrich Kemner* spoke, the church was filled to overflowing. I have never forgotten his sermon on the water flowing from the temple, Ezekiel 47. His powerful message touched me so deeply that I immediately decided to find out where this unique man came from; I had to hear him again! My path soon led to Krelingen, an idyllic village on the Heath, close to Walsrode. An outreach to the Youth of Ahlden which followed beneath the oaks of Krelingen markedly influenced my spiritual growth. Pastor *Kemner's* books often gave me great impetus and straightened out my life in no small measure.

After all these events, which led me to deeper personal Bible study, I came to the far-reaching realization that the Bible is God's Word in its entirety, and carries the absolute seal of truth. This proved to be a stable foundation, rock-solid in all situations of life and thought. Not only did I regain the simple trust in God's Word which I had known in the children's meetings, but I was so convinced of it that I was prepared to pass this on to others. At first I did this by leading Bible studies in our church district and giving personal testimonies now and then. I consider it an essential part of discipleship to belong to a Bible based congregation and to contribute personally to the ministry of that congregation.

I came to know Jesus as the Christ, the Son of God, the saviour from my lost state. He, who had been in eternity, left God the Father, became man and saved us in accordance with a plan which no intellect could have thought up. The entire New Testament testifies to the fact that God created the whole universe including this earth and all life on it through this Jesus. Nothing is exempt since "through him all things were made (= the Word, *logos* = Jesus); without him nothing was made that has been made" (John 1:3). "For by him all things were created; all things were created by him and for him" (Col 1:16).

For me, this is one of the most sublime thoughts: The Creator and the man on the cross are one and the same! What caused this Lord of Lords and King of all Kings to go to the cross for me? John 3:16 gives me the answer, though my mind cannot plumb its depths: It is His infinite Love which did everything for me so that I would not perish.

3. The Bible and Science: One subject matter in the Bible always fascinated me and that was the link between the Scriptures and scientific questions, and in particular the creation question. I realized that, for many of my intellectually orientated contemporaries, this area where intellect and faith meet is the ultimate touchstone for faith. If the theory of evolution were correct, then the creation account could not be true. But if the creation account were true then the theory of evolution would be one of the most basic and most destructive mistakes in world history. Seen from the perspective of established facts in my specialized field – information science – I came to evaluate the idea of evolution as follows: this model is not only wrong in some minor details but in its basic premise. A crucial part of life is the information given in the cells (DNA). Information, however, is not a material phenomenon, but a mental quantity which originates by a will and intelligence. New information can only originate through a process of creative thought and not through mutation or selection. This is exactly what the Bible describes in many different ways, for example in Proverbs 3:19: "By wisdom the LORD laid the earth's foundations, by understanding he set the heavens in place".

4. In the Service of Jesus: While on holiday with close friends on the North Sea island of Langeoog in 1976, the dominating topic of our talks on the beach was the creation question. My friend suggested that I share my thoughts with his congregation. So in 1977 I gave my first public talk. I was amazed that so many guests from further afield attended that evening although there had been no advertising apart from word of mouth. Obviously this was a burning issue for a lot of people. This talk resulted in more invitations to speak. During the course of the following year this ministry expanded so much nationwide that soon I could only accept a fraction of all the invitations I received.

After having read an essay in a Christian magazine in which the author combined the idea of evolution with the biblical account of Creation, I wrote my own, contrasting, Bible-oriented article on the topic. This was, however, rejected since the editor had a different "theological perspective." It was published as a pamphlet, with a co-author's contribution, in May 1977 in Brunswick with a first print run of 3000 copies. Soon after, a publishing house approached us, asking us to expand on the ideas in the pamphlet so they could be published as a paperback. This book appeared in 1978 under the title 'Creation or Evolution?'.

Through this publication, for the first time in my life, I came into contact with scientists who had a similar point of view concerning evolution and creation. Soon afterwards the study group *Wort und Wissen* (Word and Knowledge) was founded. I joined this registered association in a leading capacity in 1981. The association's goal is to make the Word of God a topic for intellectual discussion and to promote Bible-orientated science. The theory of evolution has had a lasting and detrimental influence on intellectual thinking in all areas of the natural sciences and liberal arts. Access to the Bible has been made so difficult for intellectuals in particular that they need help. After a good, hard look at the facts it becomes obvious that interpretations of scientific facts founded on the Creation account are far more realistic than interpretation attempts within the framework of the theory of evolution. For many years now I have been looking at information theory. As a result I was able to formulate some laws of nature concerning information. I have given talks on this information theory in many universities at home and abroad and hold lectures on it at scientific conferences.

Again and again people asked me to write down what I had said in my talks, so, apart from giving lectures, I finally began to write books. My second paperback 'Within 6 days from Chaos to Man' (formerly 'Logos or Chaos'), was published in 1980. Feedback from many readers confirmed that the book had helped many to turn from evolution to Creation. If somebody had told me when I was young that I would become an author, I would not have believed them. During my school years, I had a deep aversion to writing compositions or essays. If I had had a choice, I would rather have taken ten maths tests than written one composition.

In time I found that it was always the same set of important questions which were asked at the end of my lectures. I have dealt with these questions progressively in a series of paperbacks. The fact that what the Bible says can always be trusted is expounded in depth in 'So steht's geschrieben' [It is written] (1985). The book 'Das biblische Zeugnis der Schöpfung' [The Biblical Testimony of Creation] (1983) specifically shows that the Bible's statements about Creation are believable even in the light of modern scientific facts. The paperback 'If Animals Could Talk' (1990) takes a light-hearted and conversational, but scientifically based approach to Creation. The many ingenious design features of the animal kingdom are able to not only elicit amazement, but also faith. The question as to whether the many religions offer alternative paths to redemption is answered from the standpoint of the Bible in the book 'What About the Other Religions?' (1991).The necessarily closer contemplation of the Gospel that goes hand in hand with this book makes it a particularly evangelistic one. As I am told again and again, readers especially want books that relate scientific facts to the message of the Bible. These types of books have also become the focus of my writing. The books 'Stars and Their Purpose' (1993), 'In the Beginning was Information' (1994), and 'The Wonder of Man' (1996) all fall into this category. These works deal with scientific material on the basis of complete trust in the Bible, and call for faith in Christ with clear evangelistic passages.

As a result of a telephone call from a stranger in 1990, a completely different field of work opened up to me. This person explained that he was born and had studied in the Soviet Union. He is German, but speaks and writes excellent Russian. He said, "I have read several of your books. Could you envision us travelling together to the former Soviet Union and holding similar lectures there? I would translate your talks into Russian." I asked for time to think it over. The next time he called, I agreed. And so we set off on our first trip to Moscow in May 1991. For 10 days we preached the Gospel in various different places (for example, at a teacher's college, at a trade school, in hospitals, in a factory and in military barracks). God blessed the listeners with open hearts, and surprisingly many were ready to make a personal decision to turn to Jesus Christ.

The name of this fellow worker God put me alongside is Dr. Harry Tröster, who works in the development department of Mercedes Benz. Since 1990 we've made a missionary trip to the eastern bloc almost every year. Our paths led us to Moscow twice but also to Kazakhstan and Kirghizia, as well as to the (present-day Russian) northern East Prussia. We never take these trips alone, but together with well proven team. Each time, large numbers of evangelistic books, including New Testaments and children's books, are trucked beforehand to our destination.

English-speaking contries have also been on the agenda. In 1992, for example, I went on a six-week lecture tour which took me to cities in South Africa. In 1995, the tour was expanded to include Namibia as well. In 1997, I accepted an invitation to another lecture tour, this time in Australia. I held presentations in the cities of Brisbane, Darwin, Perth, Adelaide, Melbourne, Hobart (Tasmania), Sydney and Canberra.

Since 1976, I have been involved in annual tent missions. Nienhagen, a village near Celle, was my first destination. Other places included Detmold, Cologne, Schorndorf, Frankfurt-an-der-Oder, Greifswald, Zerbst, and Zwickau. The mission of 1991 will always be unforgettable, because I preached the Gospel for nine days in the Great Room of Brunswick's city hall. There, in the very place where I made my decision for Christ many years before, in 1972, I now had the privilege of calling others to follow the Lord Jesus. As my schedule has permitted, I have repeatedly taken up invitations to hold evangelistic missions in city halls, public buildings or community centres.

Looking back, I am amazed how I, a scientist, have become a preacher and author of Christian books without ever having wanted or foreseen it. The famous preacher and evangelist *Heinrich Kemner* once said: "We do not push, we are pushed." I find this to be especially true of the way God has worked in my life. God puts us into special situations. When He opens doors, walk through, because only that which God has prepared has His blessing.

Bibliography

The books written by the author are referred to in the text by the initial G, numbered consecutively, followed by the page number:

[G1] So steht's geschrieben
CLV Bielefeld*, 8th Edition 2011, 255 p

[G2] Das biblische Zeugnis der Schöpfung
SCM-Verlag, 6th Edition 1995, 188 p (out of print)

[G3] What About the Other Religions?
CLV Bielefeld*, 2nd English Edition 2001, 159 p
(11th German Edition 2014, 176 p)

[G4] In 6 Tagen vom Chaos zum Menschen
Logos oder Chaos – Naturwissenschaftliche und
biblische Grundfragen zur Schöpfung –
Aussagen zur Evolutionslehre
SCM-Verlag, 7th Edition 2007, 238 p (out of print)

[G5] In the Beginning was Information
CLV Bielefeld*, 3rd English Edition 2008, 256 p
(3rd German Edition 2002, 360 p; published by
SCM-Verlag [out of print])

[G6] Did God Use Evolution?
CLV Bielefeld*, 2nd English Edition 2001, 152 p
(8th German Edition 2009, 160 p)

[G7] Stars and Their Purpose
– Signposts in Space –
CLV Bielefeld*, 2nd English Edition 2000, 217 p
(5th German Edition 2007, 222 p)

[G8]   If Animals Could Talk
       CLV Bielefeld*, 4th English Edition 2001, 124 p
       (17th German Edition 2013, 126 p)

[G9]   The Wonder of Man
       CLV Bielefeld*, 2nd English Edition 2003, 156 p
       (2nd German Edition 2003, 155 p)

[G10] Nur die Klugen kommen ins Himmelreich
       (Interpretation of the parable of the unjust steward
       according to Luke 16:1-8), Magazine 'Bibel und
       Gemeinde', (1985), Issue 2, pp.191-208.

[G11] Time and Eternity
       CLV Bielefeld*, 1st English Edition 2001, 150 p
       (4th German Edition 2011, 155 p)

[G12] Without Excuse (W. Gitt, B. Compton, J. Fernandez)
       The Sequel to: In the Beginning was Information
       Creation Book Publisher, 1st Edition 2011, 352 p
       www.creationbookpublisher.com

[G13] Questions I Have Always Wanted to Ask
       CLV Bielefeld*, 4th English Edition 2014, 189 p
       (this book)
       (24th German Edition 2013, 192 p)

Address for ordering the books:

*   CLV Bielefeld, P.O. Box 11 01 35, 33661 Bielefeld,
    Germany, www.clv.de

Bible passages quoted verbatim are taken from the New
International Version, 1990; other versions used are indicated
in brackets after the quote.

Abbreviations Used for the Books of the Bible

Books of the Old Testament (OT)

Gen	Genesis	Eccl	Ecclesiastes
Ex	Exodus	Song	Song of Solomon
Lev	Leviticus	Is	Isaiah
Num	Numbers	Jer	Jeremiah
Deut	Deutoronomy	Lam	Lamentations
Jos	Joshua	Ez	Ezekiel
Judge	Judges	Dan	Daniel
Ruth	Ruth	Hos	Hosea
1 Sam	1 Samuel	Joel	Joel
2 Sam	2 Samuel	Amos	Amos
1 King	1 Kings	Ob	Obadiah
2 King	2 Kings	Jona	Jonah
1 Chron	1 Chronicles	Mi	Micah
2 Chron	2 Chronicles	Nah	Nahum
Ezra	Ezra	Hab	Habakuk
Neh	Nehemiah	Zeph	Zephaniah
Esther	Esther	Hag	Haggai
Job	Job	Zech	Zechariah
Ps	Psalms	Mal	Malachi
Prov	Proverbs		

Books of the New Testament (NT)

Matt	Matthew	1 Tim	1 Timothy
Mark	Mark	2 Tim	2 Timothy
Luke	Luke	Titus	Titus
John	John	Phlmn	Philemon
Acts	Acts	1 Pet	1 Peter
Rom	Romans	2 Pet	2 Peter
1 Cor	1 Corinthians	1 John	1 John
2 Cor	2 Corinthians	2 John	2 John
Gal	Galatians	3 John	3 John
Eph	Ephesians	Hebr	Hebrews
Phil	Philippians	James	James
Col	Colossians	Jude	Jude
1 Thess	1 Thessalonians	Rev	Revelation
2 Thess	2 Thessalonians		

Werner Gitt

In the Beginning was Information

256 pages, Paperback
ISBN 978-3-89397-255-5

- The origin of life from the viewpoint of information science
- What is information?
- The origin of information
- Laws of nature about information
- Languages and communication
- Is artificial intelligence possible?

These are some topics of this interesting book about information, science and the Bible.

All living organisms require information to function. If we want to make meaningful and useful statements about the origin of life, then we first have to explain what information is and how it came about. The author of this book uses many illustrative and striking examples to clarify this question.

The basic principles of information are clearly established in terms of laws and theorems which are just as valid and applicable as those employed in the natural sciences. The current materialistic representations of information are criticised, and a new model for the origin of life is derived.

Werner Gitt
Stars and Their Purpose

Signposts in Space
217 pages, Pocketbook
ISBN 978-3-89397-787-1

What expectations do you have when you start reading a book with the title "Signposts in Space"? Perhaps you think of the "little green men" which Bell and Hewish discovered when they first received signals form pulsars? Or maybe you're interested in reading something about intelligent life forms, whose existence in distant galaxies provides the material for much speculation?

Rather, in this book, we'll be looking at the effect which star systems have on us human beings. We shall answer the questions which are as fascinating as they are fundamental: What are the origins of the universe? Is its existence a coincidence or does it have predestined design? Why are there stars in this enormous universe? Who is their creator? What was the star of Bethlehem? Is it possible to have a personal relationship with this creator?

The starry sky is there for everyone and can be seen from every point on the earth. Thus this impressive scenery invites us to spend some time in reflection.

Werner Gitt

What About the Other Religions?

159 pages, Pocketbook
ISBN 978-3-89397-765-9

This book deals with a topic which often leads to heated discussions:

• There are so many religions. Are they all wrong, is there only a single correct one, or do all ultimately lead to the same goal?

• People with other religions are honest in their beliefs. They perform their prayers and sacrifices sincerely and trust fully in their religion. Surely God must also see it that way. If God is a God of love, must He not recognise all efforts to reach Him?

• Our times are characterized by understanding and tolerance. Shouldn't that also be the case between religions as Frederick the Great (1712–1786) already believed: "Everyone should be saved in his own manner"? Isn't the Gospel highly intolerant, if it throws out all other ways and claims to be uniquely correct?

These are among the questions most often asked during discussions about faith. We need real answers to help us. The author provides a thorough, Biblically-based work, which allows one to orient himself in this field of conflict.